Davies, Charles.

Bread men

$24.95

DATE			

Bread Men

CHARLES DAVIES

Bread Men

HOW THE WESTONS BUILT AN INTERNATIONAL EMPIRE

KEY PORTER·BOOKS

Canadian Cataloguing in Publication Data

Davies, Charles
  Bread men

Includes index.
ISBN 1-55013-050-1

1. George Weston Limited — History.   2. Food industry and trade — Canada — History.   3. Grocery trade — Canada — History.   4. International business enterprises — Canada — History.   I. Title.

HD9014.C34G46   1987   338.7'61664'00971   C87-094122-4

All inquiries regarding the motion picture, television and dramatic rights for this book should be addressed to the Author's representative.

  The Colbert Agency Inc.,
  303 Davenport Road,
  Toronto, Ontario M5R 1K5

Representations as to the disposition of these rights are strictly prohibited without express written consent and will be vigorously pursued to the full extent of the law.

Photo Credits
Canapress Photo Service, pages 29 and 33
The Globe & Mail, pages 36 top and bottom
Metropolitan Toronto Library Board, page 23, page 24 top, page 26 top
The Toronto Star, pages 34 and 35
The Toronto Sun, pages 28 and 32

Key Porter Books Ltd.
70 The Esplanade
Toronto, Ontario
Canada M5E 1R2

Typesetting: Imprint Typesetting
Printing and Binding: T.H. Best Printing Co. Ltd.
Printed and Bound in Canada

87 88 89 90   6 5 4 3 2 1

For Pat

Contents

Chapter One	The Empire's Flow Charts	1
Chapter Two	The Origin of the Species	19
Chapter Three	The Young Empire Builder	52
Chapter Four	A Man of Substance	66
Chapter Five	The True and Faithful Servant	85
Chapter Six	Life at the Top	102
Chapter Seven	Lifting the Veil	119
Chapter Eight	The Interregnum	135
Chapter Nine	The Making of a Conglomerateur	148
Chapter Ten	Rolling in the Aisles	164
Chapter Eleven	Waiting for Garry	173
Chapter Twelve	Plus Ça Change	188
Chronology		195
Appendix A		199
Appendix B		200
Appendix C		202
Index		205
Acknowledgements		213

Bread Men

The Empire's Flow Charts

"The grocery business is full of street people. Grocers are a tough bunch and they're not that far removed from the guys at the St. Lawrence Market who are stringing meat ... . Galen Weston is so far above them that he's kind of a regal presence, yet his whole business is built on these guys."

An acquaintance of Galen Weston
points out just how far
the family has come in two generations.

The car eased through the village of Roundwood, scarcely disturbing the Sunday morning calm. It followed a gentle S curve, a right past the parish church, a left past shops, houses and the local pub, and then up a small hill and past a stand of pine trees. About a quarter of a mile outside the village, the car pulled to a stop beside two white-painted, stone gate posts surmounted by matching statues of recumbent sheep. Seven men got out, making no sound except for the soft clasping of the car door handles as they shut. Each wore a blue mechanic's overall and carried a handgun and an Irish army-issue Gustav submachine gun. Pulling balaclavas over their heads, they moved to the gate posts. The elegant metal gates were invitingly open, and the men could see perhaps two hundred yards down a straight avenue heavily shaded by ancient beech trees. In the distance was a small patch of field with mist hanging over it. On each side of the drive was a chest-high stone fence. Beyond, to the left, they could make out gardens and, in the distance, what looked like a large pond; to the right were woods. As if they'd been rehearsing for weeks, two of the men vaulted over the fence and disappeared among the trees. The other five started to walk single file down the avenue, slowly, warily, their boots making barely a sound on the worn asphalt.

The heavy overalls quickly became oppressive. It was early in the day, but the August heat was overpowering and their weapons began to slip in their moist hands. The men came to a split in the avenue where the pavement gave way to gravel. To the left, the road arched around in a circle through trees and manicured lawns. To the right, it led to a courtyard at the back of a small two-storey stucco castle with a crenelated roof line.

It looked easy. The entrance to the courtyard was framed by the main house on the left and by a small grey stucco cottage on the right. Behind them, completing the rectangle, were white stone buildings, stables, with wrought-iron gates leading to the pasture beyond. The only sign of life was the car parked in the yard, proof that the estate's owner was home. The only palpable defences were two miniature antique cannon sitting like discarded toys on top of a small stone wall by the main house.

They walked faster now, heading into the yard so that they could break in through a rear door. But as they approached the house, a voice from the stables caused them to freeze. They were ordered to drop their guns. After a moment of incredulity and indecision, the five wheeled and fired blindly on the stable buildings. There was an instant reply as automatic weapons hissed and cracked from the windows. In seconds, more than a hundred rounds had been fired and four of the five in the yard were on the ground. They had taken bullets in the head, chest and arms. The fifth, with no place to hide, threw down his gun. The two who had been covering from the woods broke and ran, one apparently wounded as well.

As police operations go, it was a classic trap. Told by an

informant that the IRA would try to kidnap the owner of Roundwood Park and his family and to ransom them for a million pounds, an elite group of Irish anti-terrorist police, the Garda, were waiting at the estate on Sunday, August 7, 1983. Once the guns had stopped, not one of the police force was so much as wounded. In a country cursed by the terrorism spilling across its borders from Northern Ireland, this was a major victory, one that prompted the Royal Ulster Constabulary to send its heartiest congratulations. It was also the payoff for the intense anti-terrorist efforts of the Garda since the kidnapping of well-known supermarket entrepreneur Ben Dunne.

Yet even in a country where the awareness of potential violence is second nature, the idyllic estate seemed an improbable location for a gunfight. The 245-acre estate is a commercial farm where sheep are raised for export, mainly to France. It's meticulously run by a silver-haired local, Joe Sullivan, and his wife Gretta. Nestled in the hills of County Wicklow about 25 km south of Dublin and just inland from Ireland's east coast, its late eighteenth-century house and well-treed grounds afford an almost unmatched tranquillity. Residents of the area joke that, from the heights to the west of the main house, you can see England on a clear day. That may be far-fetched, but you can see serene, rolling green hills and small forests stretching to the horizon. It was this peacefulness that had attracted one of Roundwood Park's previous owners, former President of Ireland, Sean O'Kelly. It also appealed to O'Kelly's most famous postwar guest, the former supreme commander of the Allied armies in Europe, Dwight D. Eisenhower, who stopped over on his way to yet another white house.

The pastoral beauty of Roundwood Park had likewise drawn its current owner, Canadian food magnate Willard Galen Weston. Weston and his family weren't there that August weekend; they'd been warned off and were staying in England at Fort Belvedere, their storybook castle in Windsor Great Park that was once the weekend retreat of Edward VIII. In any event, Weston was playing polo that weekend at the Guards Polo Club in Windsor with the team he sponsored, the Maple Leafs, a squad of gifted amateurs and professionals whose most august member is the Prince of Wales. The IRA threat seemed far from his mind that day. He played with his typical aggression, showing the kind of fearlessness that makes his friends wonder and his wife Hilary worry. At one point in the match he was thrown from his pony, the periodic dues an enthusiast of the game has to pay, but although shaken he remounted and carried on. Asked after the match about the IRA raid, he downplayed its significance, saying that what the men wanted was to steal paintings and furnishings. Yet he also observed mordantly that the IRA hadn't done its homework: "Everyone knew I'd be in England playing polo this weekend. These matches are advertised well in advance."

There was some bravado mixed in with Weston's apparent sang-froid. He would later complain that the incident, and the subsequent two-week-long kidnapping of one of his executives in Dublin, had put his life temporarily under wraps. Never one to court publicity, he became sufficiently security-conscious that even in Toronto he took to driving a beat-up late-model car to remain inconspicuous. The incident may also have stirred unpleasant memories. In the mid-1950s, when Galen was a teenager, his father had been publicly harassed by a disaffected and somewhat deranged employee who quoted from Hitler's *Mein Kampf* and threatened to seduce Galen's six sisters. An enduring legacy of that short burst of violence in August of 1983 was that Roundwood Park was no longer a quiet family sanctuary. Although Galen has made brief, secret visits to check up on things, the rest of the family hasn't been back since.

The raid exposed Weston's Achilles' heel. Especially in Europe, where terrorism has become chillingly routine, the flip side of wealth and power is vulnerability. The fear of violence that used to be more or less the exclusive anxiety of politicians and diplomats now extends to business people — particularly business people who have celebrity status. That makes Galen Weston, with his impeccable credentials and remarkable ambitions, a prime target. The youngest of nine children, the 47-year-old Weston is the principal heir to the food processing, retailing and resources empire that was begun in 1882 by his grandfather,

Toronto baker George Weston, and then built into a globe-girdling colossus by his father, the legendary acquisitor, W. Garfield Weston. Through George Weston Ltd. of Toronto, Canada's fifth largest company in terms of sales, Galen directly controls the destiny of roughly 30 major North American companies with more than 57,000 employees that collectively generate more than $10 billion in revenues a year. And through the Associated British Foods (ABF), the conglomerate managed by his 59-year-old brother Garry, he also has a major say in the fate of another 48 companies in Europe and Australia (many of which have subsidiaries of their own), with annual revenues of roughly $7 billion.

With the possible exception of natives living in remote areas, there likely isn't a living Canadian who hasn't dealt with a Weston-owned company or used a Weston-made product. Shoppers in the Maritimes buy their weekly groceries from stores stocked by Atlantic Wholesalers, while their brethren in central and western Canada haunt the aisles of chains run by George Weston Ltd.'s best-known subsidiary, Loblaw Companies. Loblaws, Zehrs, Westfair Foods and Kelly Douglas stores all come under its banner. In any and all of them, consumers can choose from a bewildering array of Weston products. They can start their day with a shower using President's Choice soap and shampoo (just two of more than 400 products that have been developed by a rapidly growing subsidiary called Loblaw International Merchants) and then breakfast on Weston's basic white bread — still soft and chewy after all these years — or, if they're health- and diet-conscious, on a toasted slice of Fibre Goodness. Just to make sure they're getting a good start, they can pop a No Name multiple vitamin and mineral pill along with their orange juice. For lunch, they can make sandwiches using Clover Leaf tuna or salmon, with a few Amigo tortilla chips on the side, and finish off with a glass of milk and a few chocolate-covered Caramelle biscuits, one of dozens of different types that Weston's makes. To keep going through the afternoon, they can snack on Neilson Jersey Milk or Crispy Crunch chocolate bars; then at tea time they might nibble on some Cheddar Crispy Wafers or

Stoned Wheat Thins, all washed down with a cup of Twinings tea, courtesy of a subsidiary of ABF. For dinner there's always a steak from the Loblaws' meat department or some Rupert brand fish fillets for the entrée, followed by a cup of President's Blend coffee. Then a quiet time in front of a blazing President's Choice fire log, a quick brush with No Name toothpaste, the application of some White Swan toilet tissue, and off to bed.

Galen Weston isn't exceptional simply because he had the supreme good fortune to be born in the right place at the right time. As the youngest of nine children, two of whom were older brothers steeped in the family business as much if not more than he was, he could have easily drifted into self-indulgence and well-heeled insignificance. Nor is it simply that he's fabulously wealthy. Based solely on the common stock he holds in George Weston Ltd., Galen Weston is worth slightly more than $1 billion. Even without his stake in the ABF group in Britain (which, at recent stock prices and excluding shares in family holding companies and trusts, amounts to $4.8-million worth of ABF shares held in his name) and miscellaneous real estate and commercial holdings such as retailing company Holt Renfrew Ltd., he'd be one of the five richest people in Canada, and probably one of the 100 richest people on the face of the earth. Yet what's truly extraordinary about Weston is that he approaches his family business as if it were still embryonic, still in need of raw entrepreneurial guidance and development. More than 100 years and almost three generations after George Weston baked his first loaf, the head of the family empire has an undiminished predisposition to risk-taking.

It's easy to gloss over this fundamental truth, partly because Weston leads an existence that makes "Lives of the Rich and Famous" appear small-scale and banal. The occasional chukker with Prince Charles is simply the cap on a life that from the beginning has been played out in surroundings of elegant houses, fine cars and international chic. Galen and his wife, the former Irish fashion model Hilary Frayne, regularly turn up on best-dressed lists and at the most exclusive social functions; they are two of the rocks upon which social columnist Zena Cherry stands. They are associated with a list of worthy causes and institutions ranging from Toronto's Mabin School to the Ireland Fund of Canada, not to mention taking an active role in the affairs of the W. Garfield Weston Charitable Foundation set up by his father primarily to channel funds into medical research. At Weston's level of "classic, quiet wealth," as one friend of the family puts it, there really are no sectarian or social boundaries. Although Galen's background is Baptist and Methodist, he has been a sponsor of the annual charity dinner put on by the Catholic Archbishop of Toronto, Emmett Cardinal Carter. He's also known for discreet acts of kindness, such as the time he spent hours counselling and arguing with the son of Roundwood Park's manager, trying to convince the boy to attend agricultural college.

People who've met Weston tend to recall the circumstances perfectly, often with dramatic flourishes of the kind that used to be reserved for anecdotes about royal visits. Galen Weston doesn't just schlep out of his Toronto office at the end of the day; as one consultant recalls, he sweeps out of a private elevator, glides across the lobby in a floor-length sable coat accompanied by two attack-trained Doberman pinschers. His idea of a knock-about weekend jalopy is a Mercedes convertible. Galen Weston doesn't yawn and stare over your shoulder when he talks with you. He speaks in a soft, ever so slightly nasal mid-Atlantic voice and listens intently to what you have to say, as if your opinion on the state of shopping carts were the most important thing since Einstein elucidated the theory of relativity.

Weston's memorable public image is helped by his being an inch over six feet, athletically trim and costumed with casual perfection in the finest that Savile Row has to offer. In soft light, he looks as if he could be Paul McCartney's older, more refined brother. At 47, his once chubby, boyish face has become leaner, the cheekbones and the bridge of his nose more pronounced. The dazzling blond hair he had as a small child is now largely grey, but it rolls back in aristocratic waves from a clear, perfectly tanned brow. As the years have passed, in fact, he's developed an eerie resemblance to his father, the late Garfield Weston.

The style, the bearing, the intrinsic self-confidence, the good humour, the almost congenital good manners — and of course the money — have put Weston on an international social rung somewhere between the Kennedys and the Windsors. Most of the waking hours of his youth were devoted to being groomed to be what he is today, a genteel but capable entrepreneur who has assumed the mercantile equivalent of an imperial throne.

His father, Garfield Weston, was like a medieval ruler, periodically moving his court from one part of his kingdom to another, always in search of more companies to buy. After 1933, the elder Weston lived mostly in London, England, but at various times he also lived in Toronto, Vancouver and the United States. In his annual filings with the federal and provincial governments for George Weston Ltd., Garfield rarely gave the same address two years in a row. He was a staunch family man who believed in having his wife and children by his side; Galen, who was born in 1940 in wartime Britain, simply became the tail end of the family retinue. Before he enrolled at the University of Western Ontario in the late 1950s, he'd attended no fewer than 17 schools (most of which were public, since his parents felt private schools, like the British old boy network they served, were becoming a thing of the past). He'd also acquired more high-level corporate experience than most executives gain by the age of 50. Garfield Weston believed in educating his sons — but not his daughters — in the family business with a combination of humble and responsible duties. Galen followed in the footsteps of Grainger (the eldest, who'd been dispatched to Texas to run Weston interests there) and Garry (who was proving himself in his father's Australian companies) by getting his basic training fairly early. At 16, the baby of the family spent his summer in the advertising department at Loblaws Ltd. in Toronto. The next year he was toiling at Deutscher Supermarket Handels-GmbH, a chain his father had invested in in West Germany. That same year he and Garry, who was then 40, were put on the boards of George Weston Ltd. and ABF to see how things worked.

University life in quiet, conservative London, Ontario, was

pleasant — according to Galen's room-mate and future marketing wizard, David Nichol, the two of them devoted considerable
time to chasing girls — but compared with Weston's summer
jobs it was hardly exciting. Galen left school one credit shy of a
degree in business simply because he was anxious to get to the
office. "The company was pioneering the supermarket business
almost everywhere," he told an interviewer in 1981. "We were
moving. Dozens of young Canadian executives were getting into
the retail business in Europe. I wanted to get in on it."

Rather like the good and faithful servant in the parable of the
talents, Galen was given a stake by his father which he took into
the retail wilderness of the Republic of Ireland. When Galen
arrived in Dublin in the early 1960s, in fact, supermarkets and
mass merchandising techniques were practically unknown; it
was, he says, like Canada in the 1940s. Moving cautiously,
opening up less than a handful of new stores each year, he built
the Power Supermarket chain, becoming in the process a modest
real estate entrepreneur (how else could he develop store sites?),
and an investor in service and supply companies (how else could
he stock the shelves?). He also dabbled in other retail businesss,
taking a bankrupt department store and building it into the
Penney's chain and eventually buying control of another Dublin
department store, Brown, Thomas & Co. Ltd.

Weston was the closest thing to a glittering international
playboy that many Dubliners had ever seen. Often he was in the
company of Hilary Frayne, a tall, blonde model who was from a
well-to-do local family. They met in London in 1963 and dated
until 1965, when she left to study at the University of Alberta.
Not to be put off, Galen appeared on the campus the following
spring, proposed and proved to be vastly more appealing to
Hilary than textbooks. In a family known for its spectacular
nuptials, Galen's wedding was perhaps the flashiest. The two
were married on the banks of the Thames River at Henley on a
brilliantly sunny Saturday in July, 1966. For the reception, bride,
groom and guests changed into 1890s-style Klondike clothes and
then steamed down the Henley regatta course on a 90-year-old

steam-driven riverboat, the *Majestic*. In keeping with the frontier spirit, two guests — one of them a Weston executive from Ireland — got tipsy enough to fall overboard.

Weston spent almost five more years in Ireland, time to learn the finer points of retailing, to dabble in other businesses, to spend tranquil weekends at Roundwood Park, to breed polo ponies and begin the arduous struggle to become an adequate player, to develop a taste for gourmet cooking and just to be lord of the manor. In business terms, the Irish sojourn provided Galen Weston with the equivalent of an undergraduate degree; the really serious postgraduate work was waiting for him back in Toronto.

The story of Galen's corporate trial by fire has been told so many times that it has become a kind of folk tale, yet it's worth going over the basics again simply because of the magnitude of what he achieved. Under George Metcalf, an old friend and trusted lieutenant of his father who ran George Weston Ltd. from 1953 to 1967, North American operations had steadily gone into decline. Secretive, evasive and at times verging on paranoid, Metcalf, like his mentor, was an acquisitor; while president he spent more than $200 million, an incredible sum in that era, on take overs. His flaw was a lack of interest in managing his charges, new or old. Financial planning during his tenure was weak to nonexistent; in some cases subsidiaries that needed investment, such as Loblaw Groceterias in Canada and National Tea Co. in the U.S. midwest, were simply ignored. Generally speaking, most operating subsidiaries were left on their own a lot of the time. The result, by the late 1960s, was that major retail operations like Loblaws were becoming uncompetitive and other subsidiaries, such as the Sayvette department store chain and the Tamblyn drugstore chain, were suffering heavy losses. Even the food processing side of George Weston Ltd. was slipping, often because of product duplication and competition among subsidiary companies. After Metcalf was delicately nudged aside to a harmless advisory vice-presidency, Garfield Weston waited out the completion of his son's apprenticeship by using the talents of two faithful retainers, veteran accountant Keith Dalglish, and later, one of the family's and the company's principal Canadian lawyers, Ted Creber. In turn, both men improved George Weston Ltd.'s planning and financial reporting and managed to keep up a reasonable flow of revenues and profits, but neither of them tackled the really substantial problems.

Young Galen got some inkling of the scope of the empire's troubles in 1968 when his father put him on the George Weston Ltd. board. In the spring of 1971 he was called to his father's offices above Fortnum & Mason in London, asked to look over Loblaws and report back on its fate. "The big question then," he told *Business Week* in 1975, "was should this chain be closed up, or should we make the enormous investment in money and time to return it to its former place." Over the summer, Weston decided that the second answer was right and that he should be the one to pull it off. His father agreed and that fall Galen, his family and his polo ponies moved to Toronto. By February, 1972, he was Loblaw Companies' new CEO.

He spent his first year analyzing the merchandising strategies, competitiveness and cost structures of all the different companies in the Loblaw Group, and he came to the conclusion that an extensive make-over was in order. In fact, the reorganization plan that he developed for Loblaws was perhaps the most extensive ever seen in the food retailing business. Between 1973 and 1975, Weston closed down almost two-thirds of Loblaws' 1,100 supermarkets, in the process writing off more than $80 million in assets. He took Loblaws' U.S. and Canadian network of seven warehouses and consolidated them into two new facilities. Then he hired a brilliant young designer named Don Watt and put him in charge of giving Loblaws a whole new look, inside the stores and out. He approved a capital spending program of more than $40 million to expand and refurbish those supermarkets that had been considered worth keeping, as well as putting other funds into private label brands and the development of a new advertising program.

Along the way, Galen exercised what veteran food analyst Donald Tigert of Toronto's Burns Fry Ltd. calls one of his greatest strengths, "his ability to pick people." Weston already had some eminently capable advisers he'd inherited from his father. One was Roger Lindsay, a Scots accountant who had been active in guiding the fortunes of Wittington Investments Ltd., the family holding company that owns George Weston Ltd. Another was Harold W. Bailey, a venerable English lawyer who'd long served Garfield Weston as a director of ABF. Galen, however, needed a lot of new blood and he took it where he found it, whether it was from another family-owned company such as ABF, or from competing food retailers and the consulting industry. Among his biggest catches were James Watson, who was lured from the presidency of retailer Gamble-Skogmo Inc. in the United States to be chairman of National Tea Co., and Simon Reisman, former deputy minister of finance, architect of the Auto Pact, and latterly, chief negotiator in Canada's free trade talks with the United States, whom he asked to join the George Weston Ltd. board.

He found two really crucial lieutenants closer to home. One of the brightest people Galen met when he came to Canada was a young Harvard MBA graduate who had been originally hired by Weston president Ted Creber, the plump and deceptively genial-looking Richard Currie. Currie was working out of the Weston head office in the old Bank of Commerce building on King Street in Toronto, trying to solve the start-up problems for a new sugar mill. He liked to joke that he went to Harvard to learn how to think and that he took a job with the U.S.-based consulting firm of McKinsey & Co. to learn how to write the reports that would convince corporate management to take action. Actually, it was no joke. He had depth — to this day, Burns Fry chairman Peter Eby calls Currie one of the best business people in Canada — and he was tremendously persuasive. He responded to the challenge when Galen asked him to come along and help save Loblaws. Galen's other choice was the flamboyant David Nichol. After Western, Nichol had earned an undergraduate law degree at the University of British Columbia and a master's in law at Harvard. Then he too worked for McKinsey. Tall and forceful, he had a magic touch with the media and had learned a lot about the trench warfare tactics of grocery marketing. Currie would take care of the corporate structures, the financing and the serious number-crunching; Nichol would supply the style and the push that would move the products off the shelves.

Galen decided early on that he wanted to try and be an inspirational leader like his father and that, eventually, he didn't want to run either Loblaws or George Weston Ltd. full time. In the early 1970s though, the Loblaw revival was a ten-hour-a-day, six-day-a-week proposition. Throughout, Weston developed a cool, forceful style and was invariably ready to make the tough decisions. But if Weston, Currie and Nichol were the three musketeers of turnarounds, it was the latter two who often provided the inspiration. Just how true this is was evident at a party given in Toronto in the summer of 1986 at the Forest Hill home of Brian Davidson, the president of one of the Loblaw distribution companies, Intersave. The party, held in a vast tent that had been set up in the back garden, was to celebrate Currie's tenth anniversary as president of Loblaw Companies. As guests walked into the house, the first thing that caught their eyes was a large framed photograph on an easel. It showed a much younger Currie and Nichol, laughing as they looked at one another, and underneath a caption read, "It's gonna be marvellous." The two had given Weston the picture in 1972, in the lean days when Loblaws was losing millions every quarter in its major markets. Galen hung it in the foyer of his home and still remembers that it gave him great comfort.

And it *was* marvellous. First Weston conquered the supermarket aisles; then he assumed the chairmanship and presidency of the parent company. The Loblaw Group went from being the sick man of the grocery business to a market leader; these days it can claim close to a 20% share of the roughly $35 billion a year that Canadians spend on food. And as its fortunes improved, so did the parent company's. After all the paring, the consolidating, the rationalizing, the product development, the marketing and the high-profile media salesmanship, George Weston Ltd. consists of three fundamentally healthy divisions: food processing, which includes baking, milling, confectionery and candy; food distribution, which takes in the Loblaw Group as well as other major food wholesaling companies; and resources, which includes E.B. Eddy Forest Products, Eastern Fine Paper, and two fisheries companies, Connors Bros. and British Columbia Packers. Shorn of its losers, George Weston Ltd. has become what is called a balanced company. When one segment is in a cyclical decline, the others are usually on the upswing so that revenues — and profits — tend to keep growing from year to year. Since 1979, in fact, George Weston Ltd.'s revenues have risen almost 60% to an even $10 billion a year, while profits have increased by more than 55% to $118 million. Over this same period, the company's return on common equity has averaged a healthy 15.5% while the return on capital employed has generally been more than 16%.

What makes this success all the more remarkable is that Weston and his cohorts achieved their greatest victories in a business that has a veneer of civility about as thin as the cellophane wrap on a sirloin steak and where loyalties last as long as unpreserved bread. Executives in grocery chains may dress up in suits to go to the office, but their style is often as hard-nosed and streetwise as that of the dirty-aproned butchers and hawkers that you find in open-air markets. Profit margins in the grocery business typically range from 0.5% to 2% of sales. The guys at George Weston Ltd. usually manage to run a little over 1%, and they don't do it by being slow-moving cream puffs. Whether it's a question of pushing a new idea, such as the importation of all kinds of gastronomical exotica under their President's Choice private label, or embellishing an old one, such as *Dave Nichol's Insider's Report*, a refined version of a grocer's newsletter that he saw in the United States years ago, Weston group executives are, to a person, smart and pushy hustlers. In Galen Weston's case, though, the push is subdued. He can come off, as one acquaintance puts it, as "a regal presence" partly because of breeding and partly because he has people like Nichol to kick ass for him.

Having competent and aggressive managers means Weston has time for other things, just as he planned in the beginning. He can afford to take off after the Loblaw and George Weston Ltd. annual meetings in May and spend the summer in England perfecting his horsemanship and his polo swing. There is time to get involved in glitzy deals on the side, such as the purchase last year of Holt Renfrew Ltd. from Carter Hawley Hale Stores Ltd. of Los Angeles. Weston did much of his own negotiating in the $43 million Holt Renfrew deal, which he purchased mainly because he wanted an outlet for his wife's merchandising talents. Hilary Weston was active in the affairs of the family's Dublin department store, Brown, Thomas, after she and Galen were first married. Holt Renfrew, a former leader in the high-end fashion market that has declined into overpriced stodginess, will give her another chance.

In spite of his other interests, Weston remains involved in the food-oriented businesses that gave him his start. In fact, given the changes that have taken place in food retailing in recent years, changes that can turn winning companies into semi-bankrupts almost overnight, Weston — and his top managers — will have to be smarter and faster than ever to retain their edge. The Canadian grocery business, like that in the United States, has gone through a wave of mergers, acquisitions and consolidations. Thanks to the gradual break-up of one-time leader Dominion Stores Ltd. and the sell off of its assets, and such moves as U.S.-owned Canada Safeway Ltd.'s attempt to buy the food retailing arm of Woodwards Ltd. of Vancouver, the structure of the industry has been changing dramatically. In the Ontario market, for example, Loblaws remains the sales leader, and it has expanded its base by picking up some of Dominion — it paid roughly $48 million for 58 franchised Mr. Grocer stores — but it faces a newly enlarged rival in A&P which, in 1985, paid $115 million to pick up 93 of Dominion's Ontario stores. The scale of the business is changing fast too, as more companies, Loblaws included, build superstores (retail outlets of about 125,000 square feet in size compared with more traditional supermarkets, which run anywhere from 20,000 to 70,000 square feet). Many of these are volume discount outlets, but some even go that concept one better. This year, Canadians are getting their first taste of warehouse club stores, vast outlets that for an annual membership fee entitle users to even greater discounts. At the same time, more traditional retailers are building market share with the same kind of sensitivity to consumer desires that Loblaws has shown in the last decade. To take one small but telling example, when Quebec-based Super Carnaval opens its next store in the Toronto market in 1987 it will try to capitalize on the trend toward kosher meat products with a special section presided over by a resident rabbi.

All retailers are more aggressive these days, in good part because the balance of power between food suppliers and food retailers has changed too. The leverage of the "branded companies," the national brand giants such as General Foods and Nabisco, has been greatly eroded in recent years, says David Pinto, editor of the New York publication, *Mass Merchandising*. National advertising programs are less effective than they used to be; hence it's more difficult to push brand names than it was in the 1970s, he says. As well, producers' costs have accelerated, forcing them to make price concessions to retailers in order to keep their goods moving. But because of mergers and acquisitions, there are fewer and more powerful retailers to make such deals with. When those deals are made, the retailers know right down to the can or box how much they want, thanks to the extensive computer scanning equipment that monitors inventories and the flow of sales every time a granny goes through the check-out counter. If a chain doesn't like the price of your cookies, moreover, it will probably be more than happy to promote its own "house" brand instead.

It is this incredibly competitive matrix that Galen Weston contemplates from his twenty-first floor office in Toronto's Wittington Tower. His strategy for keeping Loblaws and George Weston Ltd. healthy is complex, but in essence it comes down to a long-term goal of building earnings by building assets. In 1983, Weston approved the spending of roughly $250 million to modernize the E.B. Eddy pulp mill at Espanola, Ontario. At the time, the forest industry generally was in retreat and pulp prices were depressed. In 1986, however, forest products did better, and by the end of this year, pulp prices will likely be high enough that the mill will be making money. The same long-range commitment is evident in Weston's decision in 1986 to have Loblaws spend roughly $1 billion building superstores over the next four years. Some of those new stores will be what are called discount/combination outlets; they'll have food at discount prices as well as drug- and department-store merchandise. The idea is to draw customers from the more traditional discount food stores and to head off the emerging general merchandise warehouse operators at the parking lot.

Above all, as Loblaws Ltd. president David Stewart told a retailing conference this spring, the idea is to make sure the store transcends a consumer's preferences for individual products. The key, he said, "is the retailer's ability to establish the store as the brand." At Loblaws they've done that by creating store environments and promoting house brands that quicken yuppies' pulses. At the Moore Park Loblaws in Toronto, a keynote store in the Ontario chain that neatly straddles some of the highest income residential areas in the country, the consumer satisfies his social aspirations in equal measure to his need for food.

Behind this broad strategy, Weston and his managers are remaining as selective as always, choosing the markets they'll enter — or stay in — carefully and choosing which food products they'll promote or give up on. So far they've been remarkably prescient. Loblaws pulled out of Indianapolis, where the company rightly foresaw that its position would be undermined by an emerging discount chain, but stayed in St. Louis, where it outlasted a tough battle with a major U.S. chain, Kroger Co., because it could see long-term health. Weston's food processing companies have been paid handsomely for picking some products — notably the humble Stoned Wheat Thins line of crackers — for promotion nationally in Canada and the United States. Other moves, such as obtaining the Canadian rights to Häagen-Dazs ice cream, have paid off too.

There are big risks. If a company pushes the wrong product, it wastes a lot of money. And some in the industry doubt that many places in Canada have sufficient population density to support all the superstores that competing firms, including Loblaws, seem to be building, often on adjacent corners. But the potential rewards are great. George Weston Ltd., according to veteran analyst Don Tigert, is "a beautifully positioned company that's going to have some cyclical weakness offset by superstar growth in Loblaws. Their objective is to achieve compound growth in earnings per share of 15% per annum and I think they're going to do that right through until 1990."

If that happens the least surprised person in the executive suite will be Galen Weston. His life may have been lived in lavish comfort, but it hasn't been dedicated to the idea that comfort should be taken for granted. In fact, what sets Weston apart is his persistent inclination to throw himself into risky situations and see what he can make of them. Much has changed in the 105 years since the family business was founded, but the entrepreneurial spirit remains intact.

CHAPTER 2

The Origin of the Species

"Let Butchers, Poultrers, Fishmongers contend
Each in his own trade, in what he can Defend,
Though Flesh, Fish, Whitemeat, all in fitting season,
Nourish the body, being used with reason,
Yet no man can deny (to end the strife)
Bread is worth all, being the staff of life."

from *The Mysterie and Trade*
of Baking, a seventeenth-
century English poem

It would have been hard on an adult, let alone a 12-year-old boy. In order to have fresh bread on the shelves or ready for early delivery, George Weston had to get up between three and four in the morning. Without benefit of breakfast he walked nine blocks north along a gas-lit Yonge Street to the small bake shop owned by Charles J. Frogley on the fringe of Toronto. Frogley was an independent baker, one of dozens in the city in 1876, eking out a living in his main floor shop by day and retreating exhausted to an apartment upstairs at night. From his ovens there came a daily procession of Scotch close-pan loaves, Irish batch breads, malt and rye loaves and other specialties of the era. He was more than happy to have the lean, dark-eyed boy working for him. In the pre-dawn hours he put young George to work cleaning mixing basins and building sponges, the mixtures of flour, water, yeast and sugar that were the precursors of bread dough. Before the sun was up, he had the boy hauling 120-pound sacks of flour, tending the hand-driven kneading machine and stoking the wood-fired oven.

In one friend's recollection, the young Weston was "short, but energetic." It was well he was the latter, for apprenticeship was first and foremost a test of physical endurance. It was good, too, that he was studious, because the daily routine amounted to an intensive course in the delicate chemistry of bread making. Lacking modern mechanical aids and not knowing from one day to the next whether his supplies would be of consistent quality, a baker had to be an alert craftsman who understood the nuances of mixing different flours and yeasts and the importance of maintaining ingredients at just the right temperature and with precisely the right amount of moisture. The slightest mistake could make the difference between a sweet batch that won over new customers or a spoiled one that drove regulars away.

For working like this for a minimum of ten hours a day six days a week George was paid a pittance, but he was lucky to get even that. Some fathers were actually known to pay tradesmen to take their sons on. Thanks to the basic education imparted by seven years at Toronto's Wellesley School, Weston was not, as one modern critic would incorrectly allege, a functional illiterate scarcely able to write his name. He was, however, one of the youngest in a family with seven children that was struggling to establish itself in a new country.

George's father William was already in his late forties when he came to Toronto in 1869. He and his wife Ann had originally emigrated from their native London, England, to the Lake Ontario port of Oswego, New York. William was something of a jack-of-all-trades, but Oswego proved not to be the most rewarding destination — it was a one-time English fur trading post whose growth prospects as a shipping centre had been literally by-passed by the development of the nearby Erie Canal in the mid-nineteenth century. The family's main recollection of Oswego would be that George was born there on March 23, 1865; by the time he was four, the Westons, possibly taking their cue from relatives who had gone before, moved across the lake to Oswego's historic trading rival, Toronto.

William's fortunes didn't improve all that much as a result. In his first decade in Toronto, he bounced around, working first as a labourer, then as a packer, and finally as a bookkeeper. According to family lore, some of his numerous offspring followed colourful careers. One was reputedly a ship's engineer who went to Africa in search of Dr. David Livingstone, another worked as a circus sharpshooter and yet a third was said to have been convicted of bigamy. In reality, however, William's children were mainly hard-working, God-fearing and reasonably solid citizens. One son, Joseph, became a butcher, eventually running a successful shop on Carlton Street. Two others set a particularly good example for younger brother George: Walter Weston started out as a clerk and graduated to the baking trade, while Alfred J. Weston went into the confectionery business.

Inspired by this industriousness, George bent his nose, if not to the grindstone, at least to the hearthstone. After three years with Frogley, he continued his apprenticeship with another small baker and confectioner, G.H. Bowen of Sullivan Street. Bowen widened George's education in the ways of baking, teaching him how to make everything from plain biscuits to almond cakes. By putting Weston out on bread routes through the city's western reaches, Bowen gave him his first exposure to sales and marketing; every day the teenager met his customers and developed a face-to-face understanding of what they wanted. By doing this, Bowen coincidentally provided Weston a measure of freedom and the simple pleasures of a deliveryman's life. For today's younger generations who don't even know what a breadman is, it's hard to imagine the gentle and predictable rhythms of the job. From the moment the boy hitched the horse to his dark-panelled covered cart in the morning, the day was a slow, measured ritual. The cart wound along dusty, tree-lined streets; at each stop he carried his wood and metal tray filled with an assortment of unwrapped bread and cakes up to the kitchen door. He chatted politely with matrons, indulged small children with treats, or occasionally flirted with pretty young housekeepers who exchanged tickets for bread. On he would go, plying his trade along streets where every hedge, every alleyway, every dog's hiding place, became reassuringly familiar. After the oppressive heat and sometimes cloyingly sweet aromas of the bake shop, the horsecart was a pleasure even in comparatively foul weather. In 1882, the 17-year-old scraped together enough money to buy two of Bowen's bread routes: barely in need of a shave and several years away from having the vote, George Weston was already an independent entrepreneur.

His timing couldn't have been better. Although the 1880s were generally a period of depression, Toronto was becoming the centre of an already well-developed provincial economy and was coming of age as a city. Toronto's population roughly doubled in the decade to 181,220 as the city assumed leadership of Ontario's manufacturing, financial and wholesaling industries. It was also the breeding ground for a new caste of immigrant entrepreneurs such as retailer Timothy Eaton, who used innovative methods to build a department store empire, or Peter Larkin, a wholesaler who became a millionaire on the strength of his ability to sell packaged tea.

Bread and other baked goods were harder to sell, simply because the majority of housewives made their own. There was also abundant competition. When George Weston opened for business, the city had no fewer than 58 bakers and 59 confectioners and their ranks were growing by the year. In photographs taken later in life, George Weston had a fixed, cold expression, his set lips and slightly hooded eyes suggesting a combination of inscrutability and hardness. Doubtless some of it was due to his sense of what was appropriate demeanour for a businessman of his standing. But it was also the result of the unremitting toil it took to make his fortune. As he expanded and built upon his routes, he had to be baker, bookkeeper, deliveryman, janitor and

George Weston was already becoming an important businessman in Toronto when he sat with his family for this portrait, circa 1904. From the left: George Weston, Garfield, Pearl, Gordon and Emma Maud. In front: Beatrice.

In the early 1890s George and Emma Maud Weston (lower right) posed proudly with employees outside their bread factory on Toronto's Sullivan Street.

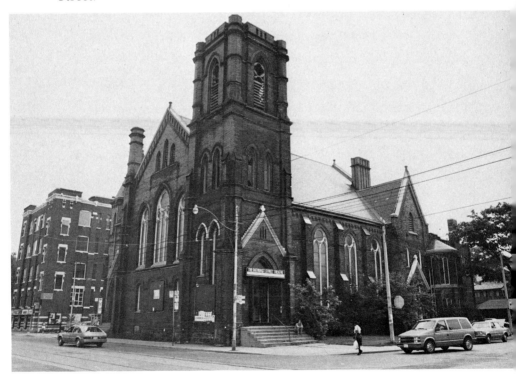

Bathurst Street Methodist Church: Now a theatre as well as a home to anti-war groups and a daycare centre, this was where Garfield first got religion.

George Weston's house on Palmerston Boulevard in Toronto. The building has long since been sold and divided into apartments, but visitors can still see George's initials preserved in the tile work in the entrance hall.

In 1917, Garfield Weston headed
for a tour of duty in the trenches
of France, and the biscuit
factories of England.

Reta Howard as a graduate of
Victoria College, class of 1920.
Garfield's future wife was gentle
and poetic.

Once he moved to England, Garfield Weston took to sending Canadian friends pictures of his ever-growing family as Christmas cards. This one was taken on the steps of "Whittington," his Marlow-on-Thames estate, in the late 1930s.

Theodore Pringle Loblaw was a poor boy from Alliston, Ontario, who struck it rich in the big city. Teaming up with another grocer, J. Milton Cork, he built Loblaw Groceterias into an important chain before his death in 1933.

Garfield Weston was 57 years old and still at the height of his power when this picture was taken in 1955. The man who had purchased London's Fortnum and Mason Ltd. four years before was still in search of newer and bigger deals.

George Metcalf was a former chocolate salesman who loved hard work, simple slogans and secrecy. Garfield Weston put him in charge of his North American holdings in the 1950s and Metcalf built a sprawling corporate giant.

A moody portrait of Garfield Weston's children taken in 1940 that is notable for the symbolism of its composition. In the centre, Garry cradles baby brother Galen in the light while their siblings remain largely unrecognizable.

Galen Weston in his Toronto headquarters with just a few of the
thousands of products that George Weston Ltd. and its various
subsidiaries either produce or sell.

Galen and Hilary Weston are at the very top of Canadian and
international society. Here they illuminate the path for the Prime
Minister and his wife Mila.

Into the breach: lawyer George Creber was loyal and tough as well as intelligent. When Garfield asked him to run things until Galen matured, he readily agreed.

Genial and soft-spoken, Keith Dalglish had the managing directorship of George Weston Ltd. suddenly thrust upon him. He lasted barely a year.

Richard Currie, here with Galen Weston at a 1986 meeting, won his spurs at Harvard and later McKinsey & Co. He's proven to be a financial wonder.

Dave Nichol, once known as "Mr. Ego" in the grocery business, has nevertheless managed to convince millions of Canadians that they need his house brand products.

George Weston Ltd.'s head office, the Wittington Tower on St. Clair
Avenue in Toronto. Inside it's leather, wood, brushed aluminum and
modern art.

Garfield Weston made a statement even with his monument in Toronto's
Mount Pleasant Cemetery. His logo is prominent, as is his favourite
saying, "Tis not the gales, but the set of your sails that determines the
way you go."

stable boy; he did everything he had to do to get ahead. And it worked. Year by year he added more routes, usually ones yielded up by less resolute competitors. He indulged in what we now know as product development, introducing in the 1890s what he called the "home-made loaf," a reasonable facsimile of its namesake that sold for pennies and convinced hundreds of women to spend less time tending their ovens.

The formula for prosperity in the bread-making business was simple. You had to out-hustle your rivals and gradually take over their customers; then you had to buy them out for the lowest amount possible. In this sense Weston was like many other late nineteenth-century businessmen, a straightforward expansionist; less than a decade after he went on his own, his two-storey plant on Sullivan Street had a staff of seven bakers, six deliverymen and two helpers. There was also a stable for the horses that pulled his six delivery wagons.

Like his competitors, he also preached quality, but he had an insider's knowledge of what people would accept and what he could get away with. As he was once overheard to remark to an inquiring foreman: "People will eat horseshit if it has enough icing on it." (A latter-day equivalent to this story is the quintessential and oft-told anecdote about his son Garfield. During a 1937 tour of Weston's new biscuit factory at Slough, England, *Maclean's* correspondent Matthew Halton noticed a small air jet that was being used to thin out the chocolate coating on biscuits at the end of the production line. Halton remarked that it was "blowing the chocolate off." "Oh no," Garfield replied, "it's blowing the profit on.") Weston was also typical in the way he treated the people who worked for him. He paid them as little as possible, just as his masters had once done with him. And since they often had less education than he did and were conditioned never to leave a job, he easily got away with it.

Although his employment practices were typical of his generation of late Victorian proprietors, Weston showed a far-sighted vision in one critical respect: he astutely realized that baking was undergoing a technological revolution. Between 1850 and 1900 it was transformed from a small-scale manual business practised in small shops to a mechanized, assembly-line one suitable for factories. By the 1890s you could import, primarily from Europe, machines that could sift flour, mix and knead dough, mold loaves and then load and unload them from a bewildering array of newly developed ovens. For a large-scale manufacturer, the British firm of Werner, Pfleiderer & Perkins Ltd. could furnish a "complete automatic bread plant" that could do all of the above and more.

In 1897 that's exactly the sort of thing George Weston was looking for. That year he opened what became known as the "Model Bakery," an imposing two-storey brick building with a corner tower that dominated the intersection of Phoebe and Soho streets in the city's Grange area. Weston now had a staff of 40, a weekly payroll of $350, and 14 horse-drawn delivery wagons. None of it was wasted. The new plant, considered the epitome of hygiene and turn-of-the-century efficiency, was capable of turning out 3,200 loaves a day.

Weston's business rapidly developed what the *Toronto Daily Star* termed "immense proportions." Within two years of opening, the Model Bakery had 30 wagons for city and suburban delivery and Weston's Home-Made Bread was available in at least 500 stores. With success came a concern for cost control, which led to his alliance with one Lawrence Spink. Spink was one of Weston's suppliers. A miller from the village of Pickering east of Toronto, he was just as interested in having an assured outlet for his flour as Weston was in having a protected source of supply. In 1900 they met, talked and decided to combine their businesses into a new one, Model Bakery Co. Ltd.

From the beginning, George Weston was the dominant partner. Model Bakery's secretary-treasurer was Charles Bodley, a trusted Weston employee, and George's wife Emma Maud and his older brother Alfred were directors. More significantly, George provided the partnership's financial muscle. He held 2,605 of the firm's 3,500 preferred shares (they had a face value of $260,500, of which he eventually paid $238,000) and he controlled virtually all of the firm's $500,000 in ordinary share capital. The only problem with this primitive exercise in corporate integration was that it didn't work. In 1905, for reasons that are unclear, Spink and Weston decided to go their separate ways. By the year end George had bought Spink's Model Bakery shares and handed back the milling assets. The bake shop was still in operation, along with the old Sullivan Street property, which George had held back from the merger, but in early 1907 Weston wound up Model Bakery Co. for good. He wasn't willing to give up total control just yet.

One evening in January, 1905, a small-time Niagara area promoter named C.R. Morden was sitting in his favourite haunt, Welland's Arlington Hotel, giving a local baker a private seminar on ways to make his company grow. The baker, one W.H. Crowther, was already well off and his sole purpose in coming to the Arlington had been to give Morden a pleasant pat on the back for his efforts in developing Welland area businesses. But here was Morden telling him between gulps of port that the only way to face the future with confidence was to consolidate, to build a network of bakeries that would span regions and, perhaps, all of Canada. If Crowther was smart, Morden said, he'd go out and take an option on every local bakery he could find. Crowther expressed polite interest, thanked Morden for his trouble and retired home, likely to ponder the folly of promoters whose reach exceeds their grasp. Morden didn't hear from Crowther again, but he was undeterred. Later that year, he tried to sell the same idea to two Regina bakers, only to be given a polite rebuff. One leading Toronto baker he approached, a successful immigrant named Mark Bredin, barely gave him the time of day. Yet off and on for the next five years Morden pushed the idea, refining plans to build large bakeries in Montreal, Toronto and London, Ontario, and even going so far as to retain a Niagara Falls architect to design and draft plans for a kind of mega-bakery in Toronto.

It was Morden, rather than his skeptical listeners, who accurately reflected the spirit of the times. Except for financial panics

in 1903 and 1907, Canada, and Toronto, had enjoyed an exceptional period of economic growth since the turn of the century.
The so-called Laurier boom, which lasted until just before the
start of the First World War, was a vast exercise in nation-
building fuelled by waves of immigration and foreign capital. But
while its most evident products were railway lines, resource
projects and power developments, it also brought new opportunities for established companies. Financial markets were now
well developed; growing ranks of bond and investment dealers
stood ready to underwrite financings for growing companies and
what they couldn't provide, banks and insurance companies
were glad to handle. What's more, the methods of financing were
becoming increasingly sophisticated, leaving managers to choose
among equity issues, bonds or various types of bank instruments
to meet their needs.

More and more often those needs had to do with mergers and
consolidations. Between 1909 and 1912, many times at the
urging of a pushy new generation of investment men from Bay
and St. James streets, no fewer than 275 companies were merged
to form 58 larger corporations. Coal, electricity, milling, paint,
shipping and textiles were all involved in major deals during this
period. Considering the hundreds of small bakeries that dotted
Canadian cities, it was unlikely that bread would be an exception.
By 1911, the persistent Morden had interested four other
partners in the idea of a bakery merger, and he'd secured options
to purchase five bakeries in Montreal, Winnipeg and Toronto,
one of which was George Weston's Model Bakery.

But Morden lacked the savvy, connections and money to put
the deal together, so that same year he sold the idea to someone
who did, a young Toronto stockbroker with impeccable refer-
ences, Cawthra Mulock. The son of a federal cabinet minister
and eminent jurist, the venerable Sir William Mulock, Cawthra
was a true blue blood, handsome and polished, right down to his
Upper Canada College education. Although only 27, he was
already a director of the Imperial Bank of Canada and the
Confederation Life Association and had ties to New York financiers. What's more, he was personally wealthy. In 1909 his aunt,

Mrs. Cawthra Murray, had left him somewhere between $4 million and $8 million.

Mulock's plan for the merger was simple. The principals of what were arguably Canada's most successful bakeries — Weston's Model Bakery along with those owned by Mark Bredin, H.C. Tomlin of Toronto and W.J. Boyd of Winnipeg — would exchange their respective assets for common and preferred stock in the new firm, to be known as Canada Bread Co., Ltd. As soon as possible the bread-and cake-making plants owned by E.J. Stuart of Montreal would be added, giving the new company a stake in the country's largest urban market. In addition to orchestrating all this, Mulock agreed to underwrite $1,250,000 in 6%, 30-year first-mortgage bonds. (In effect he used his own money to buy the bonds. Then he would resell them.) Canada Bread, according to the prospectus for its bond offering, would start life with productive assets worth $841,428 and have more than $1 million in cash sitting in the bank.

For Weston the merger had considerable appeal. At 46, he'd already made a small fortune on his own. The Model Bakery was turning in regular and healthy profits and, on a conservative basis, it had an asset value of $150,000 to $200,000. But Weston could see the trend in his industry; even though his first partnership with Spink had ended unhappily, he knew that failure to join his peers might permanently relegate his business to second-class status. Canada Bread, on the other hand, offered the hope of rapid growth and comparatively huge profits. Baking, as the company pointed out to prospective investors, was "one of the very few [industries] that is practically unaffected by bad times or periods of depression in trade." People have to eat and the new partners were optimistic enough to think they could convince the majority of Canadians to fill their bellies with the output of Canada Bread. Initially the company's plants would be able to turn out 600,000 loaves a week, but the directors expected that by quickly investing $500,000 in new plants capable of mass production, they could boost that to at least one million loaves a week before the end of the first year of operation. Within two years, they would be producing two million loaves a week.

On the strength of an audit by Price Waterhouse & Co., the company estimated that the different bakeries forming Canada Bread would have had cumulative profits of roughly $107,000 in the 1910-11 fiscal year. But in the new company's first full year of operation, profits would likely jump to $260,000, and in a few years more they'd double again to $530,000. Given the guaranteed dominance the company would have in the industry, thanks to its founding members and the improvements in mechanized baking that were coming along, how could it be otherwise?

From the first it was clear that Weston wouldn't be the one primarily responsible for making all this happen. On June 30, 1911, Weston and the other stockholders convened their first annual general meeting in Mulock's King Street offices. It was hot enough that Mulock had to open windows to get a fresh breeze for the seven starch-collared men in the room. But although he was in the chair, it was evident that the freshest person at the table was the man they unanimously elected general manager at a salary of $12,000 a year, Mark Bredin. A balding, genial-looking Irishman with a salt-and-pepper mustache that resembled a street sweeper's broom, Bredin was much like Weston, the crucial difference being that he was one step ahead in business and social stature. After emigrating to Toronto from Dublin in 1883 as a 20-year-old, Bredin went into bread making, eventually owning the largest bakery in the city. As he became successful, he also became a kind of role model for other would-be burghers. Bredin collected directorships much the way retired politicians do today; he became a member of the Canadian Manufacturers' Association and the Toronto Board of Trade and joined the National and Royal Yacht clubs. In 1908 and 1909, he even managed to find time to get elected to city council as an alderman in Ward Three.

Once skeptical about the merger, he was now an adherent determined to make it work. He exercised a management style that could best be described as eel-like. His natural tendency was to be cautious, to pursue liquidity like a religion — virtually every annual report in the 17 years he ran the company as general manager and president mentioned with pride the cash reserves stored away in the bank — but he was willing to expand, especially if there was an undervalued bakery or two lying around. In the long run, this dart-and-hide approach suited the other owners perfectly. Canada Bread was slower than expected in fulfilling its potential. By 1915, profits hit $287,000, a level they weren't to surpass for another five years. The main reason, of course, was the First World War and the supply and price disruptions that accompanied it. By the middle of the war, even though wheat was in good supply, heavy wartime demand swept the price of grain and other raw materials along on an inflationary tide. Between July, 1916, and May, 1917, the price of wheat jumped 158% to $3.10 per bushel. Similar pressures were being felt in labour costs, with the result that the price of a standard 24-ounce loaf of bread quickly doubled to 12 cents. In the 1917 annual statement, Bredin remarked on Canada Bread's ability to retain significant liquidity while doing its bit to buy war bonds, but he also gloomily noted that "during the year, our trade has passed through the greatest fluctuations of prices in modern times."

Canada Bread would survive and prosper; today, as Corporate Foods Ltd., a subsidiary of Canadian Pacific Ltd., it has annual sales of more than $100 million, and along with rival Weston Bakeries Ltd., controls roughly half of the Ontario bread market. But in its early years, the company seemed destined to face one misery after another. Although grain prices stabilized in the last year of the First World War, thanks to the regulatory efforts of the Canada Food Board in Ottawa, the company was hurt when the board abruptly changed its regulations to reduce the amount of flour substitutes allowed in each loaf. Canada Bread had just loaded up on substitutes, all of which cost more than the prevailing price of flour. And in 1919, just to add to the misery, labour strife in Montreal and Toronto pushed up operating costs while the Winnipeg General Strike depressed sales out west.

When Bredin thanked managers for their efforts in these "trying times," he wasn't kidding.

Weston was no doubt grateful for the flow of dividends that steadily came his way, even if he was saddened by the company's use of his old assets. In early 1913, the Model Bakery, a one-time paragon of modernity, was declared obsolete and was vacated. The bakery and Weston's old stables were put up for sale, along with some vacant property in Winnipeg; the asking price was $260,000. When no buyer was forthcoming, the property was leased and at one point during the First World War, it was reduced to being a storage depot and warehouse for the federal militia department. But Weston wasn't one to be overcome by sentiment. From the minute he signed the by-laws of the Canada Bread Co., he had other interests. In the company's original minutes he, along with the other founding shareholders, agreed "not to engage for a period of 10 years from May first 1911 in the business of baking, manufacturing or dealing in bread" in competition with Canada Bread, but he had hedged his bets. The minutes also show he held back "equipment and machinery pertaining to the cake and biscuit business," a reference to the factory he'd opened the year before at the corner of Richmond and Peter streets in Toronto. By 1920, when he left the board of Canada Bread and severed his ties with the company, he was running that plant quite profitably on his own.

More than six decades after his death, George Weston seems scarcely more than a stereotype of an early twentieth-century businessman. Tight-fisted and purposeful at the office, he was nevertheless highly religious and caring for his fellows, the embodiment of civic-mindedness. To all intents and purposes, he presided over a happy home populated with attractive, bright children and a dutiful wife who could rely on servants to ease the load. With the advancing years, he gathered directorships, honours and respect, and at his passing the obituary writers praised his shrewdness as well as his "unusual supply of ability and industry."

Weston was always an intensely private man — a trait he passed on to successive generations of the family — but it's fair to say that he applied industry and responsibility to his life outside work. Around 1890, he noticed that a customer on one of his bread routes had employed a new maid. She was dark-haired, with an oval face that was handsome rather than pretty, and while she seemed to lack social grace and had a harsh, slightly gritty edge to her voice, young George found her irresistible. Emma Maud Richards had been born in London, Ontario, in 1870, the daughter of an architect. Raised in the small town of Maple and later in Toronto, she'd gone into domestic service, only to find herself re-enacting a modern version of the Cinderella story. Of her courtship with George and of her hopes and dreams, we know little, and after marriage she became a quiet vessel dedicated to procreation. A daughter, Pearl, was born in 1896, followed by Garfield in 1898, George in 1899, Beatrice in 1901, Gordon in 1903 and finally Clifford in 1907.

George's growing wealth could not shield the couple from the normal trials of life. After his mother died in 1895, George gave his aging father an apartment above the Sullivan Street bakery until he too passed away in 1900, not long after the death of the infant George, who lived only two months. Business success did bring comforts in the form of bigger houses, first on St. Patrick Street and, once Canada Bread was formed, on stately Palmerston Boulevard where George and Emma lived quietly with their brood in a pillared, three-storey yellow brick mansion. By 1921 too, the family had arrived socially, rating mention in the Torontonian Society Blue Book, the "authoritative directory of elite Torontonian families." But George and his wife were hardly social — neighbours recall little evidence of parties or entertaining — and as the years passed, Emma Maud tended to be more reclusive and moody; she put on weight and took to spending her days sitting in the corner of her massive kitchen chatting idly to the housekeeper.

George may have been too busy to notice the gradual change in his wife. In fact, the more introspective and depressed she seemed, the more outward looking and genial he became. In the 1910 civic election, he followed the example set by his competitor and soon-to-be-partner, Mark Bredin, and ran for alderman in Ward Four. Weston easily outdistanced rivals George McMurrich and Albert Welch (unlike Bredin, who in the same election was defeated in his bid for a spot on the Board of Control) and was shortly, *ex officio*, elected to the board of the Victoria Industrial School as well as the board of trustees of Toronto General Hospital. The period before the First World War was a formative one in civic politics. Among the issues facing Mayor G. Reginald Geary and his newly elected council were the construction of a viaduct over the Don River Valley, the building of a new train station and the introduction of hydro-electric power to the city from Niagara Falls. A year later, city council was also asked to consider the extraordinary suggestion of a New York City firm of consulting engineers, Jacobs & Davies, Inc., that the city plunk down $23.5 million to build a subway.

Weston restrained himself to more modest projects. His first recorded act as an alderman was to propose that the Committee on Works consider "erecting one or more public lavatories at convenient points in the City." This he followed with suggestions that citizens be charged when the city had to replace private drains in the roadbed and that more park benches be installed along the lakefront at Centre Island. Weston was elected an alderman four times in all. He joined in the triumphs, such as the rowdy but happy gathering at city hall the night in 1913 when Hydro Commission chairman Adam Beck threw the switch that electrified the city; was appropriately downcast in times of sorrow such as the bout of mourning Toronto went into over the death of Edward VII in 1910; and was as naively patriotic as the next man when war was declared in 1914. He attended city council meetings almost without fail and voted on by-laws that covered every niggling aspect of urban life, but he was never a real force at city hall.

He was, however, a heavyweight at Bathurst Street Methodist

Church. In fact, as far as the parish was concerned he wasn't so much a pillar as he was the foundation. Church financial records show that between 1910 and 1924, he was consistently one of Bathurst Street Methodist's most generous supporters, contributing pew rents, large weekly offerings and underwriting the collection envelopes of his five children. After 11-year-old Clifford Weston died suddenly in 1918 — the family never referred to it, but neighbours spoke softly of an accident involving fire — George Weston continued to make offerings in his son's name. But perhaps his crowning performance in the parish was in 1910. That year, the Star Insurance Company threatened to foreclose on the church's mortgage, forcing the Reverend W.E. Pescott to start a round of fund-raising platform meetings during the regular Sunday services. As the church's history tells it, Weston, among others, "ascended the pulpit platform and called for subscriptions which were gathered by the ushers through the congregation and brought to the front, where the name and the amount were read out to the enthusiastic gathering." Moved by the moment, Weston contributed $1,000. When he kept on giving substantially, as well as throwing in extras such as a new carpet for the church's Sunday School room, others began to regard him and the family with some awe. "We were terribly impressed with their kindness to the church," recalls congregation member Margaret Robinson. "They were important people in the church."

Weston had inherited strong religious convictions from his parents, and Bathurst Street Methodist was a good place to exercise them. The church was a vigorous one in the early years of the century, boasting a congregation of nearly 400, most of whom attended regularly. It offered something for everyone. Wives could see to the affairs of the Ladies' Aid Society or the Women's Missionary Society, daughters could do good works through the Girls' Friendly Society and young men could study the Bible, sponsor foreign students or dollop on blackface to put on minstrel shows under the aegis of the Tri-Mu (Mind,

Muscles and Morals) Bible Class. For Weston the church also afforded an opportunity to indulge his businessman's acuity. As a trustee, and later a steward, of the church from 1917 to 1923, he chaired the finance committee, applying his knack for detail to everything from paying for the cleaning of boiler pipes to checking on coal deliveries.

The Methodist church, with its emphasis on hard work, sobriety and philanthropy, may have had fewer adherents than the Church of England or the Presbyterian Church in turn-of-the-century Toronto, but its standards meshed perfectly with those of the city's rising capitalist class. A list of eminent Methodists would have included the likes of the Eatons, the Masseys and the Flavelles. Weston wasn't on their social plateau to be sure, and his donations may have been comparatively small potatoes, but he was on the right track.

Like other businessmen of his generation, he was also deeply interested in producing a successor. When Clifford died in 1918, Weston became depressed and considered selling out entirely. His second youngest, Gordon, was still a teenager and, in any event, he showed considerably more interest in drawing and painting than in the business. Garfield, his eldest son, showed the most potential, but he had gone overseas in 1917 to serve with the Canadian Army Engineers in France. When he came back in 1919 and went into the firm, all he seemed to want to do was spend large amounts of money to begin production of what he was sure would be a hot product in the 1920s, "English quality" biscuits.

One evening in early March, 1924, Weston decided to walk home from his factory in a spring snowstorm. The following day he had a cold, and within a week it had begun to deteriorate into pneumonia. By the first week of April he could no longer rise from his bed. While the world outside revelled in the exploits of Babe Ruth, who had just capped spring training by sending a ball over the 436-foot mark at Yankee Stadium, and wondered at the bile of a young German war veteran named Adolf Hitler, who had just been jailed following an abortive putsch, Weston spent his waning strength fretting about the fate of his business. On April 7, a cool, cloudy day, he spoke his last, telling Emma Maud that he worried his children might not measure up and that Garfield in particular just didn't know how to handle money.

CHAPTER 3

The Young Empire Builder

> *"From just meeting him, you would never think of him as the magnate that he turned out to be. Garfield was a nice chap, good looking, and he had an English motor car."*
>
> Charles E. Durand, a
> friend of Garfield Weston
> in the 1920s

Garfield Weston returned from the First World War having learned two essential lessons. The first, which he shared with all the other survivors, was an intimate knowledge of the depths to which humankind can sink in wartime. He left for the trenches of France with the Canadian Army Engineers in 1917, looking, according to a description given by one of his officers, "young and pale and fragile." But determined. His hair close-cropped in the strictest military fashion, his chin square and his mouth set with the wry, ever so slightly truculent twist that would become his trademark, young Garfield gave a good account of himself. In the end though, he was less impressed by the mud and blood of day-to-day soldiering than by an immense business opportunity he managed to identify in his spare time.

On one of his leaves in England, Weston joined a group of Canadian soldiers who were invited to tour one of the country's leading biscuit factories. He wasn't prepared for the sheer scale of the factory. Here was a modern, assembly-line operation capable of belching out millions of biscuits every week and then shipping them off in brightly decorated tins and boxes to British and overseas markets. A good British biscuit, the plant managers told him, could, if shipped properly in a tin, arrive months later in darkest Africa or, for that matter, in the northern Canadian bush, as fresh and flavourful as it had been the moment it came out of the oven. The experience made his father's seven-year-old Toronto factory with its cracker-barrel bulk approach seem dated and trifling by comparison.

The story of this tour and the ones he arranged on his own on subsequent leaves to England sound like the concoction of some overly fanciful public relations man bent on explaining his master's business triumphs. One has an image of Weston and his friends alighting from a train in a cavernous London station, their grimy puttees and battle jackets replaced by dress uniforms; while his chums head for the fleshpots and pubs of the city, Garfield checks out the local cookie company. Legend has it that Weston made a point, when talking to soldiers from other parts of the Empire, of asking about biscuits and how well they sold in different countries. According to Charles Durand, a retired banker who was a friend of Weston's in the 1920s, he was a straightforward, outgoing and personable young man who saw an objective and proceeded to chase it. There was an opportunity; he was in a position to do some research, so why not?

In fact, it wasn't quite that simple. The real problem in evaluating Garfield Weston's long and richly accomplished business life is boiling off all the mythology that surrounded it, much of which was contributed by Garfield Weston himself. It was as if his becoming the world's largest baker somehow created a responsibility, perhaps even a compulsion, to set all the events of his life in a flattering context, to stick basically to the truth but, with rare exceptions, to refrain publicly from telling all of it. In his seventies, Weston confided in the wife of one of his executives over lunch in his private fourth-floor dining room at Fortnum & Mason. He told her that his time away from the trenches during the Great War hadn't always been a series of brilliantly successful market research field trips. At one point, he recalled, he received a shocking letter from his father telling him first that his 11-year-old brother Clifford had died, and second, that his father was depressed enough as a result to consider selling out. Here Garfield was, sensing opportunity, yet thousands of miles away there was a tragedy with consequences that, except for the tenuous and delayed contact provided by sea mail, he was powerless to do anything about. He wrote back telling his father to hang on, to wait for this apparently interminable war to be over so that Garfield could come home.

The elder Weston did hang on, but when Garfield returned to Toronto in 1919, he discovered that his father was in no mood to entertain any bright ideas for expansion. Markets had remained buoyant after the war; the biscuit factory was doing reasonably well and Weston's interest in Canada Bread Co. was paying off handsomely. But the war had made it harder to get supplies, and prices kept rising. The coming of peace just seemed to add to the economic stresses already created by the war boom. When things finally ground to a halt and recession hit in mid-1920, across Canada the manufacturing and financial sectors felt the pain. The veteran baker was grateful to be in the food business, comforting himself with the knowledge that come what may, people had to eat — and they would prefer bread to biscuits. George Weston was, Durand recalls, "wrapped in bread." He was also in his mid-fifties and tired. Retirement was beginning to look good.

His son Garfield was altogether different. Now 21, he had resumed the apprenticeship that had been interrupted by the war and was energetically working his way through the various departments of the family company. He also had this grandiose

idea. The raw materials for quality biscuit production — "English quality," as Garfield would later say — were all
in Ontario: wheat, flour, butter and milk that were equal to any
found in the world. What was needed was equipment and
expertise, and these he proposed to buy overseas.

If Garfield Weston wasn't above applying a little confectioner's
icing to the events of his life, he certainly wasn't above using
them to make a point either. Take his birth, for example. Weston
loved to tell everyone that he was "born in the smell of bread" in
an apartment over his father's shop, a humble myth that
overlooked the fact that by the time he arrived, his father was
financially sound and the family no longer lived over the work-
place. But occasionally he could go even further. During the
Second World War, he recounted in England an episode that
glorified his own salesmanship for the benefit of visiting Canadian financial journalist, Floyd Chalmers. Weston told Chalmers
about a call he made in the 1920s to find shelf space for the output
of his newly formed Weston Biscuit Co. He went to see Bill
Pentland, the president of Dominion Stores, whose office happened to be in the building at Peter and Sullivan streets where
Weston had come into the world. Weston wanted Pentland to
increase the number of biscuit boxes from the four that each
Dominion was then carrying, but neither his charm nor his
already considerable persuasiveness could budge the grocery
executive. Abruptly and without explanation, Weston got up and
began to walk around the room, looking at the walls.

"What are you looking for?" asked Pentland, puzzled.

"I was born in this room in 1898," Weston explained. "It was
my parents' bedroom over the bake shop. The doctor who
delivered me says that when I was just a few minutes old, I did
something rude and splattered the wall. I'm trying to find that
spot because it would remind me that when I was a newborn, I
expressed exactly what I now feel about Bill Pentland and his
Dominion Stores."

Pentland had a sense of humour. He laughed and promised

Weston that he would put eight tins of his biscuits in every Dominion outlet.

According to the Toronto City Directory in 1898, Weston's parents were in fact living in somewhat pleasanter surroundings on nearby St. Patrick Street. It's likely that the odoriferous apartment above the bake shop was then occupied by Garfield's aging and recently widowed grandfather, William Weston. It's conceivable that the smell of bread could have wafted several blocks to the newborn's nostrils, but Weston, an instinctive storyteller, seems to have realized that the truth could have compromised the romance of his version.

Garfield Weston is remembered by the few people still alive who knew him as a youth as outgoing, playful, loyal and when the occasion demanded, quite fearless. Once when he was about 12, a neighbour recalls, he quickly dealt with two older boys who he felt were trying to take advantage of his sister, Pearl. They didn't repeat the offence. All the boy's qualities were enhanced by the fact that he was an extrovert in a family that was more withdrawn. At church, or along the quiet, treed confines of Palmerston Boulevard, the Weston children played well with friends but knew when to keep them at arm's length. Few got much farther than the kitchen.

The young Weston was imbued with his father's natural discipline and with the stiff Wesleyan values endorsed by the Bathurst Street Methodist Church. To the southwest of the church's sanctuary, for example, there was a Sunday School room designed in the so-called "Akron style." It was an open two-storey room that resembled an Elizabethan theatre. It had a small raised stage on one side from which the superintendent, who in Garfield's boyhood was one Ernest Davidge, watched anywhere from 15 to 20 different classes being conducted in a semi-circle arrangement of small tiered cells on two levels, each separated from the other by hinged wood partitions you could pull down like the cover of a roll-top desk. Should Garfield or one of his chums so much as cross his eyes, retribution from Davidge came like a thunderbolt from God.

Like his sisters, Garfield was academically bright; he earned good marks at King Edward Senior School and at Harbord Collegiate Institute, where he eschewed technical and business courses in favour of those leading to matriculation. In the second form (the equivalent of the modern Grade 10), he stood fourth in the class at Christmas and eighth in June. In his fourth form, which was his last year of formal education, he stood twelfth at Christmas. He was more than an academic drudge, though. He boxed at Harbord — at least long enough to get his nose broken — and he proudly wore the orange and black colours as a member of the school's junior and senior football teams. Visitors to the school can still see a photo of the 1915 team on the wall, with Garfield triumphantly holding the ball, even though he wasn't the captain. That was just one indicator that Weston had something special, a style that made him a natural leader. Another was his performance as the first vice-president of Harbord's Senior Literary Society. On October 21, 1915, he took part in the school's Trafalgar Day festivities, a celebration of the 110th anniversary of Lord Horatio Nelson's brilliant naval victory over the French and Spanish in the Napoleonic wars. After the students in the Harbord assembly hall had kicked things off with a spirited rendition of "Rule Britannia," and one Lavell Norris of the fourth form had played "The Death of Nelson" on his euphonium, there came, to use the words of the society's recording secretary Helen Kirkwood, the *"pièce de résistance* of the meeting — the Trafalgar Day Oration by Mr. Garfield Weston of Form IV B, who had been chosen as Trafalgar Day orator. The choice of his form and the staff was justified by the splendidly vivid portrayal he gave of the Battle of Trafalgar. He explained the day, and why we celebrate it, and his handling of the subject was masterful. Mr. Weston's speech was fittingly followed by a piano duet by Miss Fraser and Miss Richardson — 'We'll Never Let The Old Flag Fall'."

And neither would Weston. Again, according to legend, Garfield's class was given an equally rousing speech by a teacher in the fall of 1915 on the need to defeat the dreaded Hun. It was said to be so convincing that all the boys in the class practically ran down to the recruitment office. This sounds plausible. At that stage of the war, public feeling was just beginning to shift from naive patriotism to grief and dismay. Canadian casualties were beginning to mount, particularly after the second battle of Ypres that spring; singing and flag-waving had given way to more pragmatic demonstrations such as sock-knitting and efforts by assorted civic groups and associations to raise funds to buy machine guns to send to their boys at the front. Germans increasingly were being depicted as monsters; they'd used poison gas for the first time at Ypres; they'd sunk an apparently innocent ocean liner, the *Lusitania*, off the Irish coast; and then they had executed a dedicated Canadian nurse, Edith Cavell, for suspected espionage. Clearly they deserved the worst that Canada's young men could mete out.

But according to Garfield's daughter, Miriam Weston Burnett, the patriotism wasn't quite so pure or so well organized. The principal of Harbord, one Colonel Hagarty, was given to badgering students about their duty to King and Country and suggesting to them that it was less than fitting to sit on their rears getting an education when their brethren were going over the top. Regular doses of guilt so shamed Garfield that he left school at the end of 1915 intending to enlist. The only problem, as he discovered when he spoke to a recruiting officer, was that because he was only 17, he needed his father's permission. His father wouldn't co-operate, but he did give Garfield a job at the biscuit factory, which kept him occupied until his eighteenth birthday on February 26. Now he could sign up on his own.

Before Garfield went overseas, he'd been quite literally working from the ground up, starting by cleaning out the stalls of the horses which pulled his father's delivery wagons. Once he returned, however, he moved quickly through the ranks, rising by 1924 to general manager. Expansion was hard work, made easier by the fact that even at this stage Weston had the ability to think on the grand scale. Once he'd convinced his father, after a heated argument, that a move into large-scale biscuit production was worthwhile, he returned to England and arranged to buy the machinery that could do it; he wanted the best, most up-to-date equipment so he could surmount the production inefficiencies he could see plaguing English factories. He also scoured the country for the managers and technicians who could make it all work. Eventually, he hired a number and paid to relocate them and their families to Canada (a resettlement scheme which, oddly enough, he would reverse after the Second World War by sending young supermarket managers to the United Kingdom). The big problem, from the first, was money. Weston was constantly visiting bankers, who were then, as now, not given to heavy-duty risk-taking. In fact, of all the financial institutions in Toronto, only the Bank of Nova Scotia was willing to take a chance on the young entrepreneur.

Despite his headlong plunge into business, Weston managed to find time for a social life. His sister Pearl, who was working towards an arts degree at Victoria College at the University of Toronto, introduced him to one of her friends and classmates, Reta Lila Howard. Weston was charmed. Howard was pretty rather than beautiful, with soft features and reddish brown hair that was cut short with bangs across her forehead. She was bright and talented and sensitive. At Victoria she sang in the Ladies Choral Club and was elected official poetess of the class executive (Pearl Weston was treasurer) in her graduating year, 1919-20. To top things off she came from a Methodist background. Her family, though, seemed to have always been on the move; Reta had attended Jarvis Collegiate Institute in Toronto, but her parents had lived in Victoria, British Columbia; Burk's Falls, Ontario; and finally Moose Jaw, Saskatchewan.

With the exception of a couple of brief stories that were written about her during the Second World War and when she died in 1967, scarcely anything was ever publicly known about Reta Howard. Not even the cause of her death has been disclosed. For all intents and purposes, she was the archetype of a magnate's supportive wife, backing her husband's statements on everything from the virtues of a public education to the need to revitalize the tired financial heart of the Empire with bright young men from the colonies. Later in life, Garfield Weston told friends he had decided while a young man that he wanted a large family — ten children to be exact. His wife certainly did her best to acquiesce, eventually bearing him nine. Reta did, however, test his mettle by moving back to Moose Jaw with her family after she graduated, prompting Garfield to tell his surprised parents that he was going to head west and marry her there. To the irritation of his parents, who were denied an opportunity for a proper Toronto wedding, this is just what he did in 1921, taking Reta as his wife in the Howard back yard while the Wedding March was played by his bride's close friend, Elizabeth Bogue.

The next few years were pleasant ones. Even though business was suffering hard times, people were still willing to buy Weston's biscuits, especially the successful "English-style" ones he introduced in 1922. After 1921, George Weston's agreement with the other founders of Canada Bread expired and the family was able to get back to baking. Garfield was made a vice-president of the company in 1921, manager of the biscuit plant the following year, and general manager the year after that. He had now worked in virtually every part of the business and had proven himself capable of taking on major projects such as the installation of the company's own creamery (to produce butter for the production line), as well as successfully designing a series of advertisements with Dickensian illustrations to drive home the old-world standard of his product. In their off hours, Garfield and his young wife played tennis or motored around in his large English-made automobile. They also went on picnics with Elizabeth Bogue, who by then had finished her music studies at the Royal Conservatory, and her new husband, Charles Durand.

To some observers, Garfield Weston's blazing ascent was scarcely disturbed by his father's unexpected death in the spring of 1924. In fact, his father's passing seemed to propel him forward, evidenced by the inspiring grave-side proclamation he supposedly made about spreading the family name around the globe or at least throughout the British Empire. "[Garfield Weston] values his family name above all else, and as long as the Weston name is associated with the biscuit industry, it will stand for English standards of quality," rhapsodized *Canadian Grocer* in 1926. "Mr. Weston is perpetuating his father's name by building up an enduring monument, built on the rock of quality and founded on the spirit of a greater Canadian Nation. The dream desire of a young Canadian has now become a reality." Exactly what Garfield Weston may have said at his father's funeral isn't clear, but at the time the dream desire was actually quavering. Weston, quite naturally, was in shock; his father may have opposed him on expansion in some respects, but he was vastly more experienced than his son. Garfield was also frightened enough to pray for guidance. "He had had little education; he felt stupid and inadequate to the responsibility that had fallen on him," his daughter Wendy recalled in the 1960s. "He felt that he couldn't carry it alone, and he asked for God's help. He believes that he got definite guidance at that time and that he has never lacked it since. He seeks it before every important move."

In those early years, Weston knew intuitively not to show any sign of weakness to associates or subordinates. In fact, he quickly demonstrated that he was a master at projecting unfettered self-confidence. Jack Duggan, a retired baker, started working for Weston as a teenager in the plant on Dupont Street in Toronto in 1931. He vividly recalls the tough work, the long hours and the weekly visits Garfield Weston made to the plant: "He was young, blond and successful; he was well put together. He may not have been six feet tall but he looked that way to me ... . He just exuded confidence and success."

Some of Garfield's confidence was deserved. The company had profits of $25,000 the year he took over; by 1926, with economic growth resuming, they had grown to $85,000. In this early period he was also gradually gaining control of the family's corporate affairs. By the early 1930s, his younger brother Gordon, now a self-proclaimed artist, was listed as a director of one of the family companies, George Weston Bread & Cakes

Ltd., while Pearl, now Mrs. Stanley Robertson, and Beatrice, now Mrs. Ernest Ashbourne, were stockholders. None of them, however, was really active in making operating decisions or planning for the future. As of 1928, Garfield Weston was effectively in charge and in January that year he incorporated George Weston Ltd. as a federal, publicly traded company. The move was a smart one: the new company bought the bread and biscuit businesses from him, leaving him not only in control but, thanks to the fact that George Weston Ltd. was listed on the stock exchange, with access to considerably more equity than before. What's more, the new company could claim immediate success. With the economy and business now humming again, it reported sales for 1928 of $3 million and net income of $167,597.

His self-confidence rising with every passing sales objective, Weston was beginning to think big, perhaps too big. By May of that year, he'd used part of his capital to buy William Paterson Ltd., a 65-year-old biscuit and confectionery manufacturer in Brantford, Ontario. Then, with backing from a New York financier, he set up his first U.S. company, George Weston Biscuit Co., with plants at Watertown, Massachusetts, and Passaic, New Jersey. He got them up and running just in time to welcome the Crash of 1929 with cookies and milk. Having committed himself to his first major investment in expansion, he came to the numbing realization that the biscuit industry was badly over-built. Once markets turned down at the onset of the Depression, revenues dried up faster than cream filling on a summer's day.

"It was an awful cropper," he admitted years later. "I went almost bankrupt and had a physical breakdown too. But it was the most profitable breakdown any man ever had. It was my formative year. I learned then that courage is the vital element in life. I developed a duodenal ulcer and had to go to a hospital in Boston. During my convalescence I bought 20 or 30 of the finest books I could find in biography and history and I studied them. It was worthwhile. Something came to me then; I went back to Canada a failure, but a different man. I remodelled my methods completely and then I started to rebuild my fortunes in the United States."

Modern management theorists who preach that a tilt through bankruptcy proceedings is a valuable learning experience have nothing on Garfield Weston. Few people can take a debilitating brush with total failure and make it seem like an inspirational visit to a spa. Moreover, he began to understand as he tossed and turned on his hospital bed that his expansion wasn't so much wrong as it was mistimed. Instead of opening costly new plants in peaking markets, he should have waited until the downturn and then looked for cheap assets. Wellington Jeffers, a *Financial Post* correspondent at the time, reported: "The crash, which is a disaster to most people affected by it, appeared in the light of an opportunity to Garfield Weston. After a year or more of intensive study of its various aspects, he began to argue strongly and impressively with fellow executives and associates that there never had been and never would be as great an opportunity to buy into other promising businesses. He believed that never again in this generation would there be opportunities as great to buy up excellent plants at liquidation prices."

Most of his fellow executives thought he might have spent too long in a hot bake shop. Factory ownership, whatever the price, was useless if there was no one to buy your production. But this hardly deterred Weston. Back in Toronto he firmed up his control over the family holdings, arranging through George Weston Ltd. to buy control of the still privately held George Weston Bread & Cakes. By doing this, he also brought two previous Ontario bakery acquisitions, Lawlor's Bread and Regal Bakeries, under the public company. Then, in 1931, he used William Paterson preference shares to buy control of the Independent Biscuit Co. Ltd. of Calgary, Alberta. Late that year, he also spent $65,000 ($25,000 in cash and a $40,000 five-year mortgage) to buy Ontario Bakeries Ltd., which gave him seven more bakeries spread across southern and central Ontario. The deal indicates just how far Weston was already ahead of his more traditional competitors. Ontario Bakeries had been formed only in the late

1920s, a fearful amalgamation of small operators who were concerned about containing rising costs. Once they banded together, they failed to put any real effort into consolidating and rationalizing, leaving them easy prey for the young take over artist.

Weston's bankers were predictably leery of advancing more funds, especially when he divulged his real target: the aging bakeries and biscuit factories of England. For any economically informed person in 1933, the idea of buying British assets of any description verged on sheer insanity. Not even the staunchest Empire booster could deny that the trade-dependent Mother Country was being hammered unmercifully by the Depression. Unemployment, which had run at about the one million mark through the late 1920s, was now at roughly three and a half million. A financial crisis in March, 1931, in which Britain's underlying financial solvency was questioned, led directly to the replacement of Ramsay MacDonald's Labour government by a coalition National Government blending Labour, Conservative and Liberal ministers. With the economy in a shambles and traditional party affiliations shattered, the cranks started coming out of the woodwork. Two press barons, Lord Rothermere and Lord Beaverbrook — a transplanted Canadian who became Garfield Weston's hero during the Second World War — used their papers to scream for protectionism, then they banded together to form what they called the United Empire Party, which promoted the creation of a British Empire free trade bloc, protected by a high tariff wall.

Toronto bankers who were disinclined to fund new bakeries in places like Guelph, Ontario, could hardly be expected to throw their money into such a financial sinkhole, no matter how cheap the acquisitions might be. Weston, on the other hand, had sufficient belief in Britain's investment possibilities that he paid a bakery expert the equivalent of £2,000 a year to go over and evaluate prospects. The problem was that he couldn't find anyone in Canada seriously willing to contemplate such a scheme, even when he dressed it up with the notion that a large number of Canadian-controlled bakeries overseas would make fine customers for Canadian grain. His last card was one he'd played before, almost disastrously, in the late 1920s. He went again to New York, this time looking for investors who had been smart enough to sell short — borrow stock, sell it and then buy it back at a much lower price to return it to its original owner — before the Crash. Weston told an interviewer with *Fortune* magazine in the 1960s that he paid a stock market tip-sheet writer $10,000 to set up a meeting with some well-heeled speculators who could stake him to $2 million. The tipster delivered three of the best, including the famous Bernard E. Smith, known as "Sell 'em Ben" because of his predilection for dumping shares the instant the U.S. government made an optimistic economic statement.

"While I talked, they just sat there never moving a muscle," Weston recalled. "One said something against it. Another said, 'Why England? If it was a U.S. business I might go along with you on it.' I told them now was the time to put some money outside the country and England was a sound investment. Then Smith spoke up. He said, 'What's the good of asking all these questions? I'm gonna buy this guy's stock. Send it around tomorrow and you'll have your cheque. Any of the rest of you can buy in at the same price.' He never asked the amount or the price. I went over to shake his hand. I looked him in the eye and said, 'I'll make you a lot of money.' And I did."

As the next few decades would prove, it was no more than Garfield Weston was willing to do for himself.

CHAPTER 4

A Man of Substance

> *"Yet I don't want money. I'm not quite sure what the dream is, but it's not a selfish one. Perhaps it's patriotic. I want the British Empire to be happy, safe and prosperous."*
>
> Garfield Weston quoted in
> the *Toronto Star Weekly,*
> June 11, 1938

May 11, 1951. The absolute pinnacle of Garfield Weston's business life, his moment at the Everest of economic achievement, was that day, when he gained control of a smallish but venerable Piccadilly provisioner, Fortnum & Mason Ltd. The upstart baker's son from the colonies was suddenly calling the shots at the exquisite seven-floor store where clerks in frock coats filled aristocratic hampers with everything from Beluga caviar to kangaroo-tail soup, a store that had looked after the weekend shopping for Britain's kings and queens for more than 250 years.

On the surface, it didn't seem like much of a triumph. Weston's gradual purchase of Fortnum's stock over the previous two months had unfortunately coincided with an internal battle among several of the company's directors. It was as if a noble family had suddenly decided to air their dirty laundry in public, and their actions embarrassed everyone involved, particularly Weston. In purely financial terms, there wasn't really anything in the deal for him. He paid about $1 million for control, but for Britain's largest baker and biscuit maker, and Canada's largest baker and grocer, this was no longer an impressive sum. And Fortnum's annual profits, which in 1950 amounted to $364,924, would be virtually invisible on the collective Weston bottom line. As he told a gaggle of reporters who accosted him as he was boarding a New York flight at London's airport that evening, "The acquisition will not give me another thousand a year income."

It did, however, give him legitimacy, a confirmation of his status as one of Britain's leading men of business, a man who stood for the betterment of the Empire as much as, if not more than, for the increase of his personal wealth. Neither a knighthood nor a lesser honour was forthcoming after the 18 years he had spent in Britain (and given the casual criticisms he'd periodically levelled at Britain's old boy network and "caste" system, such recognition could hardly have been expected), so owning the nobility's general store would have to do. In another sense, the Fortnum purchase marked his final maturation as a businessman, the ultimate refinement of a brash huckster into a seasoned industrial potentate. He'd been saying for years that if you had pluck and got on with things you could get ahead. And if he now seemed reclusive and inclined to dispense simplistic maxims to explain his success rather than to seek out the media and indulge in the headline-grabbing theatrics of old, perhaps experience had taught him a few lessons along the way.

In November, 1938, Garfield Weston had just completed his thirtieth British plant, a biscuit factory at Newport, a small city near Cardiff in South Wales. Weston was proud of his accomplishment, because he'd found a way to make money and provide jobs in a part of the United Kingdom where economic depression still held most people in its grip. A standard plant opening with plump local officials, forelock-tugging workers and inconsequential speeches followed by polite gloved applause simply would not do. What the occasion needed, as Weston would have put it, was some good Canadian pep. His solution was to rent a 12-car passenger train, which he then proceeded to fill with roughly 200 prominent business people, including the man who had loaned him the money to build the plant in the first place, the automotive baron of Britain, Lord Nuffield. Weston's guests walked along a red carpet in Paddington Station to board a train that must have made many self-conscious in the extreme: the front of the steam locomotive was covered with a giant shield that proclaimed: "Weston Biscuits Special — Work Harder for Britain," a slogan that was repeated along the side of each car. In every window there was a Union Jack, giving the whole thing the appearance of a victorious troop train returning from a foreign triumph.

Weston had taken care of the details at the other end as well. The local station platform was again covered in red carpet and the mayor was on hand to attend the Board of Trade regiment that would alight and then go by motorcade to the plant. To add to the occasion, Weston had hired a few brass bands and his Worship had seen to it that there was a suitably large crowd of no fewer than 30,000 slightly puzzled but suitably grateful Welsh folk along the motorcade route. By the time Weston ascended the podium at the factory, a mere opening ceremony had been elevated into part political rally and part Last Night of the Proms. "I am the greatest living exponent of enthusiasm in this country," Weston told his listeners, "and I want every soul to be sold on the idea of working harder for Britain, just as my salesmen are enthused by me to sell my biscuits." The crowd cheered.

The Newport opening showed that turning the ordinary into the extraordinary was becoming Weston's style. So was his conscious and often brilliant effort to equate the needs of business, and especially *his* business, with the needs of country and Empire. Weston had already demonstrated an ability to make a corporate take over seem like a kindly, fraternal act; it was only natural that he find a way to turn biscuit baking into an expression of high patriotism. His upbringing, his wartime experiences and now his life in Britain were confirmation of the value of the Empire. The British Empire was thought by its adherents to be one of the greatest cultural and, coincidentally, economic forces in the world, and here he was sharing in it, contributing to it. His belief in the quality of his products and the efficiency with which he could produce them was absolute. It's little wonder that the lines between corporate culture and the wider culture quite easily blurred in his mind.

In his seventies, Weston would look back on his acquisitive middle years and say, "We just grew like Topsy," giving the impression that growth had happened randomly, that he was no more than an instinctive, seat-of-the-pants entrepreneur who kept stumbling across the irresistible corporate bargains that dotted the Mother Country. Weston did have great instincts, in part because he was a natural contrarian who went against prevailing business wisdom, but his success was based on more than luck and happenstance. His assault on Britain was, in fact, thoroughly modern and calculated.

As early as the First World War, Weston had concluded that the way to make high-quality biscuits profitably was on a large-scale, assembly-line basis. Henry Ford and Lord Nuffield had the right idea; now he was going to apply mass production to food. But in 1933 he sat in his Toronto office thumbing through a one-inch-thick consultant's report on the British biscuit industry that spelled out everything except what he wanted to read. The report, which had ended up costing him $10,000, gave him chapter and verse about public tastes across the British Isles and it itemized the strengths and weaknesses of his potential competitors, starting with the giants, such as Peek Frean, and working down to small family operations. In all there were 120 biscuit firms in operation, seven of them major national concerns that were well entrenched. The report's advice was simple and to the point: don't go.

Weston wasn't convinced. He had a map of Britain put up in his office that had all the biscuit makers marked on it, colour coded with different inks to denote whether they were small, medium or large producers. As he stared at it he kept coming back to the same fact. Although the big seven were vastly larger than their competitors, together they still didn't account for more than 60% of the industry's annual volume. "I knew there was no monopoly and that I couldn't be done in by price cutting," he recalled later. "I knew that if I introduced my methods and modern equipment I had a gold mine. And in fact it was easier than I thought."

Symbolically, he started at the top of the map, with a respected, 150-year-old producer, Mitchell & Muil Ltd. of Aberdeen. The canny owners at Mitchell & Muil must scarcely have been able to restrain their glee when in 1934 the sleek, fast-talking Weston walked in and asked to buy their biscuit division. That part of the company had been running at a loss for some time and, with its obsolete equipment, the prospect for a return to profits was slight. They were only too delighted to sell. They must have been equally surprised when Weston quickly announced that he was shutting down the Aberdeen plant and moving the operation to a new factory in Edinburgh. His economic rationale was simplicity itself. He now owned a venerable name, and his research told him that on average it cost a major producer roughly one shilling to produce a biscuit. He planned modern plants that would do the same for sixpence.

Within a year, he was doing just that. He'd also begun construction of his second major plant, this time at the Slough Trading Estate, west of London in Buckinghamshire. By early 1937 he would be on his way to a third, this time in Belfast, Northern Ireland. Along the way he seemed to pick up small bakeries quite literally by the dozen. Starting in 1934 with an old London firm, Chibnall's Bakeries, he spent roughly two years acquiring and gradually modernizing 15 companies which in

1936 he grouped together in a new firm, Allied Bakeries Ltd. By 1937, Weston had roughly 5,000 employees producing bread, biscuits and confectionery with collective sales of more than £3 million a year. Weston was already Britain's second largest purchaser of flour and other baking materials after the Co-operative Wholesale Society. The estimated asset value of these British holdings had grown from zero to £2.5 million and, happily for investors who purchased stock in Allied Bakeries at the outset, the value of their equity had risen by more than 50%.

In one sense, this rapid growth wasn't really all that astonishing. Despite the worst fears of the nay-sayers on Bay and Wall streets, who had initially cautioned Weston to stay close to the roost, his decision to begin investing in Britain in 1933 was prescient. After the misery that attended the panic two years before and the seeming inability of the national government to do much of anything about it beyond feeble, underfunded public works projects, economic recovery was slowly and surely setting in. The recovery wasn't yet a broad or massive turnaround in Britain's fortunes; it was confined mainly to domestic industries such as building, particularly house building, related industries such as home furnishings and appliances, and emerging companies in what would have been considered the high-tech industries of the day — cars, chemicals and radios. International trade was still in the doldrums. Yet between the winter of 1932 and early 1935, the unemployment rolls were shaved from more than three million people to fewer than two million and industrial production levels made steady gains. Combined with generally falling price levels, this meant that even those still on the dole were better off.

As Weston realized, even the unemployed have to eat, and he could see how his salesman's charm might give him the means to put more biscuits and loaves on their tables. In fact, as London's *Daily Express* intimated in a 1938 feature, he might even have taken advantage of a few doddering proprietors in reaching this objective. "He has collected bakeries as some men collect stamps," the newspaper wrote. "There was a joke that he couldn't go out in the afternoon without coming home with a couple of bakeries. He bought them largely from oldish men with no sons who felt doubtful about the future. He would pick his man; find out everything about his family, hobbies and idiosyncrasies, then approach him with 100% high pressure enthusiasm and personality, bounded on all sides by humility, tact, and above all, great friendliness. He acted almost like a son to them." Weston never confirmed the story that one elderly baker had offered to officially adopt him, but he did admit that he had benefited greatly from the fact that the First World War had eliminated much of a generation of young men. And in the end he wasn't inclined to run roughshod over the feelings of their bereaved parents. "Once convinced of my sincerity they were marvellous," he said at the time. "You see, they couldn't find one single thing in my past against me and that's helpful. They were merely a bit hurt and annoyed until I went to them and made friends."

Weston's personal appeal was one of his most effective assets. Whether it was with an important business figure whose advice or financing he sought, or a journalist who could provide positive rather than critical coverage, his style was outgoing, friendly and generous of spirit. At one point in the mid-1930s, recalls former *Financial Post* editor Floyd Chalmers, Weston called on him to complain about an article that seemed critical of a recent corporate move. Weston didn't yell; he didn't threaten legal action; he didn't throw insults. He did, however, casually point out to Chalmers that the deal the newspaper had heaped abuse on had been given the stamp of approval by two titans of Canadian business Weston had consulted beforehand, Colonel Sam McLaughlin of General Motors and Sam Moore of Moore Business Forms. Could Chalmers take issue with two of the best business brains in the land? "I commended him on getting such solid advice," Chalmers recalls with amusement.

Weston courted the rich and prominent in Britain as well and, increasingly, he came away with their money as well as their advice. To get it, he was willing to endure even the more bizarre eccentricities of some of his famous patrons. Once, for example, he called on Joseph Rank, then the world's largest miller and easily one of the five richest men in England. Rank was over 90 but still an ardent student of phrenology who was eager to massage Weston's carefully groomed head for signs of intelligence and character. Evidently he found many, for he is reported to have told his sons after a lengthy interview with Weston that the young Canadian was "a comer" and that they should do anything they could to hire him.

Weston didn't excel merely in private interviews. As his Welsh biscuit train more than amply proved, he had considerable abilities when it came to pomp and circumstance. Once a year he gathered his executives and sales force for a banquet in London to which he was also careful to invite assorted bankers, investors and other powerful business contacts. The 1937 meeting was held just before Christmas at the Savoy Hotel and featured an Arabian Nights show and a closing speech by Weston himself to the several hundred guests. In the description of one who heard him, his impact was nothing short of astounding. "The actual words of his speech, with a few exceptions, hardly remain in my memory. It was merely a speech about business, and how successful they had all been, and how much more successful they were all going to be in the future, and how fine it was to work together, and how grand it was to have deals in business and all that. But the manner of it was magnetism itself. The man gave off personality, sincerity, and people felt he was saying tremendous new, important things. 'I am a man with a dream,' he said, and tears came into the eyes of wealthy, hardened, sophisticated men."

Journalists gradually developed an immense battery of adjectives to describe Weston, ranging from the mundane — "dynamite," "high explosive" and "mustard and vinegar" — to the egregious — "a romantic with a golden touch." They strove to portray his dynamism and restless energy: "He would pass in a tube train for what he is, a salesman," one wrote. "His hair is brushed back from an intelligent but not domed brow. His nose looks as though he had played rugby — and he has, through boxing, broken it. His mouth is like Charles Laughton's, though never sardonic. His eyes are bright and alive and so is his whole being." The one thing writers could never agree on was his height. He was described as either a strapping six-footer or as so dwarf-like that he would insist on standing while his interviewer sat. The best guess is that he was about five feet, ten inches.

Weston, for his part, was more than willing to play to the press in the 1930s, to captivate them and hold forth on everything from the price of wheat to his ultimate desires. "You surely don't think I'm in business to make money, do you?" he once asked CBC and *Maclean's* correspondent, Matthew Halton. No, he continued, his real objective was a better and stronger British Empire. He also satisfied Halton's curiosity about his professed spiritualism. "Sometimes," Weston said, "I do feel I'm tuning into something, I don't know what. After all, I don't think I could have done all this alone."

But much of it he did. By the time he was 40, Weston had developed formidable management skills; in fact, many of the hottest principles of managing in the 1970s and 1980s are precepts he followed as a matter of course. First and foremost, Weston understood that he was responsible for setting and communicating the goals and methods of his companies, what we now euphemistically refer to as corporate culture. CEOs who seek public forums or make their own product commercials are merely repeating tactics Garfield Weston tried 40 years ago, such as this song he got his publicists to crank out in the late 1930s:

You tackle your job, I'll tackle mine,
Each in our own good way.
Courage and pep in our eye and our step,
Drive dull care away.
Forward, yes forward, with main and might,
Shoulder to shoulder, the goal's in sight.
For we'll soon be on top of the world all right,
And that's where we mean to stay.

Hokey yes, but then Irving Berlin had declined Weston's $5,000 offer to pen a similarly inspirational number.

Likewise, the effort modern executives make to stay in touch with operations, what we call "management by walking around," is what Weston was doing from the late 1920s on, when he instituted weekly visits to his Canadian bread plants. After Allied Bakeries was established, Weston kept on the move and made sure that everyone who worked for him did too. Virtually every day in his office at Slough Estates, he gathered his top officials for working lunches, putting his products to the acid test even while he pressed his top officials to be "like terriers in their unself-consciousness," to find ways to boost sales and profits.

One way to help the latter was the relentless pursuit of efficiency. "Suppose you've got a small bakery business that uses 200 sacks of flour a week," he said. "You'll have to pay, say, $5 a sack. But look what happens if you have a 50,000 sack business. Buying flour on that scale you can get it for $4 a sack. You're making $50,000 a week just by doing a bigger business." In his case, that flour increasingly came from Canada. Weston's early scheme to import the rich grain of the Dominion, which more seasoned businessmen had written off as a young man's naive foolishness, had actually taken root. Likewise, Weston was invariably willing to invest in the best equipment, but because he was a competitive — some felt predatory — price cutter who undersold other firms by as much as 50%, he had to keep it going round the clock. His decision to run three shifts a day at many of his factories in the late 1930s wasn't so much a grab at market dominance as it was a necessary move to generate the cash to pay for capital improvements and earn a satisfactory return on investment.

Weston's aggressive retailing practices, initially a novelty in Britain, had gradually become a necessary habit because there were many in his industry who would have cheerfully baked him in one of his own ovens. Weston had, in fact, upset the fundamental order of things in British baking. Before his arrival, the industry had been dominated by two large private millers, Rank and Spillers, and by the Co-operative Wholesale Society which supplied flour to the smaller Co-operative Retail Societies that accounted for about one-quarter of Britain's bread production. By buying up bakeries and having them use Canadian flour, Weston was systematically cutting off the outlets of the established milling interests. Rank and Spillers, who had previously dabbled in bakery investments, usually when one of their customers could no longer afford to pay for his flour shipments, responded by going on a bakery-buying spree of their own, the former creating British Bakeries and the latter United Bakeries. Old Joseph Rank had been prophetic in his desire to sign up Weston. Even though both groups went on to thrive, Weston's intrusion meant they had to fight harder than ever to make sales. The big losers in the new order were the co-operative societies. Although they had pioneered modern baking technology as well as door-to-door delivery, they were ill-managed and failed to invest in modernization with the large cash surpluses they earned in the years before the Second World War. Between 1935 and 1945, their overall market share dropped from 25% to 18%.

Weston's invasion of British baking had another interesting by-product. It helped to coalesce organized labour in the industry, changing it from a loose federation of 17 district unions into one national organization. By forcing the industry to combine into fewer units, Weston made it possible for the union to cover its needs with fewer agreements; eventually there would be one keynote agreement struck with the Wholesale & Multiple Federation of Master Bakers (composed of bakeries owned by Rank, Spillers and the co-operatives) that set the national tone. Despite the fact that Weston companies almost invariably showed themselves to be progressive on such issues as wages, fringe benefits, working conditions and pensions, organized labour always regarded Weston with deep suspicion at best. In 1967, a profile of Weston and his companies prepared by the International Union of Food & Allied Workers in Geneva took pains to see his career in a negative light. His impact on baking in Britain was interpreted as a mean-spirited conquest worthy of a robber baron even though, as the profile admitted, it benefited workers mightily in the end. The final indignity was the blatantly incorrect assertion by the report's author, Ernest Haynes, the then president of the Bakers' Union of England and Wales, that Weston was "the only son of a French-Canadian engineer."

In the 1930s, however, union men weren't the only ones leery of the brash Canadian. In July, 1938, Maclean Publishing Co. president Horace T. Hunter wrote an internal memorandum to *Maclean's* editor Napier Moore expressing his reservations:

I checked up further with sources whose opinion should be worth something both from the bakery end and the financial end. The information I get is that they are in a good deal of a quandary regarding him. They believe he is more interested in the stock market than he is in the business itself. Ben Smith, who is an out-and-out speculator, went in with him in connection with some of his operations in Great Britain, but I understand Weston has put it over him and he has withdrawn. Weston is very ambitious and a great publicity seeker. It is felt, however, his operations have been on such a speculative basis that considerable time will have to elapse before men in the financial or bakery business will have any confidence in him.

Moore passed along a copy to Floyd Chalmers at the *Financial Post* and got a more up-to-date and realistic assessment in reply:

Weston is a very likeable fellow. He is indeed ambitious and in order to achieve his objectives as quickly as possible he is prepared to undertake speculative financial operations which would never be considered by the more conservative type of financial or business man.

This may lead to the impression that he is more interested in the stock market than he is in the business itself. I have never gathered this impression from my many conversations with him and my observations of his operations. I think he is building up a tremendous business as the means of acquiring wealth and power. I think he would like to become another Lord Beaverbrook, be a Member of Parliament, own newspapers, and be

looked up to as a genius and a man of influence and achievement
.... I think he holds the view quite candidly that as long as he can
make money for big men they will stay along with him. He took
certain influential Britishers into his company in England and has
made a great deal of money for them. He told me that in many
cases he didn't need their money and did not particularly value
their advice. But he knew that if he could make money for them
they would have faith and confidence in him. The day would
come when their influence would be of value to him, he said. I
imagine he was looking forward to a title and to political
preferment ... .

Don't dismiss Weston as a failure yet, nor be too confident in
forecasting his ultimate downfall. He may come a cropper, but
each year that passes puts some solid flesh on the rapidly
growing skeleton of his enterprises.

By natural inclination, Weston was building a personal life that
couldn't help but endear him to Britons. After he moved his
family to Britain in 1935, he bought a 200-acre estate at Marlow-
on-Thames in Buckinghamshire, within easy commuting distance of his offices at Slough. He named his new home "Whittington" after the legendary fourteenth-century character Dick
Whittington, a poor lad who became one of the richest men in
England thanks in part to his cat's prowess at catching plague-
ridden rats. (Garfield Weston would later drop the "h" and name
his family's holding company Wittington.) The estate was the
former home of Lord Devonport and nicely situated in an area
traditionally favoured by the aristocracy for their country
retreats. Whittington had history — stone cut on the property
had gone into the building of Windsor Castle — and well-known
appointments, including a large rock garden, that kept a staff of
five groundsmen running from morning to night. With tongue
in cheek Weston could have argued that he needed the acreage
and its half mile of frontage along the Thames just to provide the
room for his ever-growing family. Between 1923, when the
eldest child, Miriam, was born, and 1940, when the youngest,

Galen, arrived, Reta Howard Weston entered the delivery room about once every 22 months. Friends joked that Whittington's ornamental lake had once featured a statue of a stork which Weston replaced with the less fertile image of a stone swan.

To all of his children, Garfield Weston was a proud and doting father. He avoided London social engagements, preferring to follow a rigid nine-to-five work schedule and to keep his weekends free to be with the children. On the grounds of the estate he played with them, taught them to ride ponies and poke around the gardens. Although his estate was nearly in the shadow of Eton, Weston had determined that his children should go to day schools so they would not become party to the irrelevancies of upper-class English life. As Reta Weston explained, "Now if my sons went to Eton, with their father successful in business, they'd be 'safe.' But we won't have that. We feel they get more out of a day school, living at home and getting to know their father and his business. The public schools of England have no understanding of twentieth-century life. Fifty years ago they were all right, perhaps. But what do their masters know of life today or teach them of world affairs?" Arguably, this was reverse snobbery at its worst, but Weston was willing to be seduced by other familial trappings of vast success. In 1936, he immortalized his then seven children in the best English tradition by having Ethel Everett of the Royal Academy paint a group portrait of them clustered around their mother. The story went round that one aging baker who had previously met Weston was so moved by the painting when it briefly went on exhibition that he decided to sell his business to the Canadian.

Floyd Chalmers had been right to perceive that Weston ultimately sought political preferment, just as Weston's friend Charles Durand had many years before. Still, just why or how Weston ended up as a British member of Parliament after the 1939 election isn't totally clear. Weston once tried to explain it away by saying that Winston Churchill had tabbed him for the House of Lords and suggested a stint in the lower house to get basic experience in the workings of government. Churchill, of course, didn't become prime minister until May, 1940, but it seems possible that Neville Chamberlain and others in the government at the outbreak of war the previous September could have sensed Weston's potential worth. He was now an established force in business who was wealthy and well connected. And compared with many of the nation's aging tycoons, he gave infinitely more promise of making a positive contribution to the supremely difficult task of defeating Germany.

In the event, he didn't exactly run for Parliament. Under a wartime political truce, the three major parties — the Conservatives, Labour and Liberals — agreed in the 1939 election to simply replace or reconfirm members in the various ridings, leaving overall party standings as they were. Weston stood unopposed in the Midlands riding of Macclesfield, a largely working-class district with roots in the silk trade. He replaced J.R. Remer, a now sickly 21-year veteran of the Commons who cheerfully predicted that the new boy would "take up a great position in the councils of state." Given his own views on the feebleness of the upper classes and the need to break down the traditional social barriers of the nation, the choice of riding was only too appropriate.

There's not much evidence that Weston ever spent much of his time either in the House or in the riding. Nor is there much to suggest a particularly eminent role in the conduct of the war. He did, however, have his uses. One was as a high-level courier on runs from London to Washington and Ottawa, charged with ensuring there was a steady flow of food supplies across the Atlantic to the blockaded Mother Country. And perhaps an even more important role, which oddly enough was initiated by the reluctant aggressor Chamberlain, was as a propagandist. The British government concluded in the early days of the war that Americans, and Canadians for that matter, failed to appreciate the gravity of the danger or the phenomenal effort being made by the British forces, especially the Royal Air Force, to hang on. After mid-June 1940 when the Germans overran France, it was literally Britain against the Axis powers. Thus, when Weston alighted from his frequent Atlantic Clipper flights he was more than happy to make speeches outlining everything from the brilliance of Canadian military leaders such as General Andrew McNaughton to the efficacy of the Maginot Line (he spoke too soon) and Hitler's classic stupidity in invading Norway in early 1940. This German move, in Weston's assessment, meant that the war would likely be over in a year. On the other hand, he told North American audiences, "Britain hasn't made a single mistake in the conduct of the war to date, but by failing to provide adequate information about her successes has allowed a flood of German propaganda to splash gloom across this continent."

This was a palpable exaggeration, given the real tension and gloom that spread across Britain in the summer of 1940. The Battle of Britain, waged in the air over the English Channel in those few warm bright days, has been justifiably included with Trafalgar and Waterloo as one of the key military turning points in British life. And while Weston was clearly too old to join the "few" who climbed into the cockpits of Hurricanes and Spitfires to batter daily the waves of fighters sent by the Luftwaffe, he responded to the need of the time with generosity and his customary flamboyance. On the afternoon of August 15, after a week of heavy German air raids and spectacular aerial battles, Weston was found hunkered over the Commons news ticker, waiting for dispatches and counting up the day's gains and losses. Roughly 400 German planes had joined in the three waves that had attacked since the morning. By evening the ticker flashed the outcome: 61 confirmed kills of German aircraft and only 16 British planes lost. Weston was exhilarated, so much so that the following day he raced to the office of Lord Beaverbrook, the Minister of Aircraft Production. Beaverbrook was involved in intense discussion with his aide Brendan Bracken in a corridor when Weston briskly came up and offered to pay $445,000 to replace all the lost planes.

Weston was immensely glad to be an imperial benefactor. He was a true believer in the Empire's cause and it was doubly satisfying to be able to make the gesture to Beaverbrook, a man who undoubtedly was one of his great idols. Beaverbrook, a Presbyterian minister's son from Newcastle, New Brunswick, was a perfect role model for Weston. From humble origins, he'd become one of Canada's premier financiers and merger specialists before moving to Britain before the First World War. He successively became a newspaper baron, cabinet minister and all-round political force. Now in Britain's most trying hour, he, in his role as Minister of Aircraft Production, was second only to Churchill in importance. Weston was so enamoured of Beaverbrook's success that he could be heard throughout the war talking about acquiring his own chain of newspapers.

Weston never became a confidant of Beaverbrook, but he was conspicuously generous on other occasions, donating everything from radios for Canadian troops to $50,000 to kick off Beaverbrook's new Speed-the-Tanks Fund after the latter was made Minister of Supply in 1941. That summer the British press carried a photo of three of Weston's children perched on a spanking new tank with the name "Garfield Weston" stencilled across the front. Unfortunately Britain didn't need the money so much as productive capacity. The massive donations, as both Beaverbrook and Weston realized, were really no more than good publicity for the war effort.

Such was Weston's support for Beaverbrook that the minister's resignation in early 1942 prompted him to make his first and only address in the House of Commons. His speech on February 25 took but a few minutes. It amounted to a plea for Beaverbrook's return to the cabinet and cast doubt on the expressed reason — chronic asthma — for his resignation. "I do not believe, however, that that is why he left," Weston told the honourable members. "I believe, and I am entitled to express my personal belief, that Lord Beaverbrook left because he had become sick unto death of government by committee." In other words, the government's ablest minister, "the Empire's greatest individual driving force at the present time," had been stifled by petty bureaucrats. This was only partly true. Beaverbrook had run roughshod over other departments and had constantly battled bureaucratic mentalities, particularly the top brass at the Air Ministry. But it was also fair to note that Beaverbrook had fundamental differences with Churchill and had never intended to run any ministry on a long-term basis.

Weston never forgot about business or acquisitions, even at the height of the war. The quintessential story of his eye for a bargain concerns his chance meeting with R.B. Bennett on a flight to Canada in 1943. Bennett, who had been conspicuously unsuccessful as Canada's prime minister during the Depression, was now Viscount Bennett (courtesy of his old friend Beaverbrook), spending his time inflicting his "rotund oratory," as historian A.J.P. Taylor described it, on British armament factory managers. Weston, however, was less interested in news from the factories than he was in talking about the gemstone of Bennett's personal corporate holdings, his controlling interest in the E.B. Eddy Company of Hull, Quebec. Bennett had inherited his Eddy stock from a friend of his youth, Jennie Shirreff, the second wife of founder Ezra Butler Eddy, and her brother Harry Shirreff. Bennett had no great attachment to the fortunes of the company, but Weston could sense potential. Eddy's pulp and paper production could be tied directly to the packaging of Weston food products, and by-products such as cellulose might have an enormous impact on newly developing businesses such as plastics. Before the plane landed, a deal that would eventually see Weston take control of E.B. Eddy for roughly $4 million was taking shape.

Weston's wartime trips encompassed as many business functions as political/propaganda appointments and they gradually reinforced in Weston's mind that his future lay in corporate life rather than the House of Commons. In 1944, he was on the buy-out trail again, this time gaining control of the Winnipeg-based food wholesaler, Western Grocers Ltd. (a controversial move at the time because not all of Western's stockholders were consulted about the purchase). At war's end, Weston abruptly moved back to Canada, buying the Vancouver estate of financier

Austin C. Taylor. For the next five years he was constantly on the move, seeing to the affairs of his growing North American and British interests and making periodic acquisitions, most notably food retailer Loblaws Ltd. in 1947 and candymaker William Neilson Co. in 1948.

By early 1951 there didn't seem to be that many worlds left to conquer. But when two directors of Fortnum & Mason approached him and asked if he might be interested in buying their shares, he couldn't resist. Unfortunately one of those directors was Ernest Thornton-Smith, who was just coming under fire from his fellow board members for his ownership of stock in gin producer Seager Evans, then under investigation by the London Stock Exchange because of alleged improper trading. When the stock exchange probe was announced in March, Fortnum chairman Colonel Ian Anderson and two others on the board asked Thornton-Smith to resign. Weston, who was gradually buying more stock and had come onto the board along with his son Garry, was caught squarely in the middle of the fight. Thornton-Smith eventually went, and at a shareholders' meeting on May 4, Weston had all the shares he needed for a coronation. The only sour note was the criticism that Fortnum should have been sold to an Englishman. "Don't you consider me British?" Weston asked the meeting. "I take great exception to the criticism that I should not come in because I am a Canadian."

CHAPTER 5

The True and Faithful Servant

"The secret of life is to think big, believe big, pray big, act big, hope big—and big results will come."

George C. Metcalf, 1962

As far as anyone knows, George Metcalf has never intended to write his memoirs. Although his more than 60-year business career is one of the more accomplished in Canadian history and his days as head of Loblaws and later of its parent, George Weston Ltd., allowed him to dominate the grocery trade to an extent that no one before or since has managed to equal, talking about his achievements would be a violation of the operating principle he applied almost as much to his loved ones as to his associates: a desire for secrecy. Even at the end of a long working day, sitting in front of the television or propped up in bed listening to one of his beloved opera records, Metcalf wasn't inclined to let down his guard. "My father didn't talk a great deal at home about business," his son, George Metcalf, Jr., recalls. "My father played his life that way, pretty close to the vest."

Nor has he ever formally retired. Although rendered an invalid by Parkinson's disease and unable to communicate, the 83-year-old Metcalf is still listed as the honorary chairman of George Weston Ltd.'s food distributing and retailing subsidiary, Loblaw Companies Ltd. While he was reduced to an advisory vice-presidency after he surrendered his posts as George Weston Ltd.'s president and managing director in 1967, until a few years ago he was still reporting for work at 6 A.M. It was as if he had become the exemplar of the management slogan he had used to inspire literally thousands of Loblaw executives over the decades, "Finish Right."

Thanks to his extraordinary drive and loyalty, he became Garfield Weston's trusted regent. Weston made a practice of hiring the best management talents he could find on both sides of the Atlantic, and even then he often found them wanting. If you stumbled you were gone; if you produced, you prospered. After 1947, when Weston first bought into Loblaws, Metcalf, more than any other individual, was responsible for the growth and health of North American operations. In this Metcalf not only prospered but also ended up making many of the decisions that turned Loblaws and George Weston Ltd. into sprawling conglomerates in the fifties and sixties. When the full extent of Metcalf's empire-building for Weston was revealed in 1966, the investment community, not to mention Loblaws' and George Weston Ltd.'s stockholders, were amazed. "Garfield Weston may own the complex," an associate noted, "but George runs it. He's a financial genius and Weston seems to have unlimited faith in him."

Although there may have been little physical resemblance between the two — Metcalf was a diminutive featherweight, an assertive Huck Finn in horn rims with a moonbeam smile — they had much in common. Both were intensely religious; they shared much the same patriotic outlook on the virtues of the Dominion and the need to preserve the British Empire. Ultimately, neither was able to distinguish between love of country and love of business. Likewise, both were intensely private family men, although in Metcalf's case work tended to intrude more into his personal life. Finally, their most important common characteristics were their high degree of motivation and their desire to sell and do deals. For both men, the idea of going a whole week without engaging in some business act would have been unthinkable.

There was one major difference between the two: if Garfield Weston was born with a silver spoon in his mouth, Metcalf's was scrap metal. Metcalf was born in Manchester, England, on January 9, 1904, the first of ten children fathered by Charles Metcalf, who came from a well-to-do Midlands family that had interests in the textile trade as well as dyeworks. An older sister had a thriving retail clothing business with shops in London and Paris. Metcalf senior, however, wanted none of it. For reasons now obscure to his descendants, he left home as a teenager and enlisted in the British Army in time to fight in the Boer War. When the war ended in 1902 he married his sweetheart, Mabel Atkins, and settled down to an uneventful spell of child rearing and odd jobs. By 1908, restless and with his prospects scarcely improved, he convinced his wife to emigrate to Canada. Once the couple were settled in Toronto's west end, however, their lot scarcely improved. Charles Metcalf worked at a variety of jobs before settling down as a groom employed in the private stables of the wealthy. When his patrons gradually traded in their horses for motorcars, he got a driver's licence and became a chauffeur.

Chauffeuring did not measure up to the excitement of soldiering, and George, at the age of 11, and his now numerous siblings were treated to the sight of their father enlisting in the Canadian Army to do his bit in the Great War. This time he didn't make the front lines; he was instead reduced to the role of training sergeant stiffening younger recruits for the unknown perils awaiting them overseas. Charles Metcalf, in fact, never learned to say no to a good war. In 1939, after lying about his age, the now overweight and balding veteran somehow convinced the army to take him again. He was assigned to work as a cook at Camp Borden until his officers discovered he was over 60 and arranged to give him an honourable discharge.

Given such a role model, and the financial realities of raising a large family, young George didn't waste much time before getting down to practicalities. He was given a rudimentary education, the equivalent of grade seven or eight, and at age 16, he got his first full-time job, as a stockboy in the Gladstone Avenue plant of William Neilson Ltd. It was 1920 and the beginning of the only truly carefree part of Metcalf's life. Neilson in those days was a magic place, a family-owned and -run concern that daily turned out tons of ice cream (it was then Canada's largest producer) and boxed chocolates. The boy's duties gave him time to explore a thriving business whose self-sufficiency would be impossibly uneconomic today. In its eight-year-old brick factory, Neilson made its own ice — 90 tons a day — ice cream tins, wooden pails and boxes for ice cream bricks and candies. A separate department handled the printing and embossing for all the company's packages. Neilson even supplied customized wooden ice cream coolers to its retail customers.

Metcalf liked his employers and gradually developed a strong sense of loyalty to William Neilson and the three sons who helped him run the business. What's more, the job was relatively secure. Cool, damp summers might dim the prospects for ice cream, but there was always a stable market for soft centres. As William Neilson had quaintly put it on the eve of the First World War, "I am of the opinion that the business will continue to show large expansion and the returns therefrom will show continued improvement." Outside work, Metcalf led an active life. He was becoming well known as a local athlete, playing soccer as well as semi-professional baseball evenings and weekends. And despite the fact that he was only five foot seven inches and weighed just 135 pounds, he was an accomplished boxer. "He was a good fighter, but he had a short reach," his son George, Jr., says. "He won most of his fights, but he took a lot of punishment."

Some of the teams Metcalf played on in the early 1920s were run by the youth groups at Carman United Church on Sheridan Avenue in Toronto's west end. He had joined the church during a tumultuous period of change. In 1924, a few years after he had started attending, the United Church emerged from the union of Canada's Congregationalist, Methodist and Presbyterian churches to become Canada's largest Protestant denomination. Metcalf came to adore church music, a considerable progression from the English music-hall songs he'd grown up with and this enjoyment led him to an interest in and a deep love of opera. Metcalf loved to sing and in later life he would sometimes express regret that his baritone voice hadn't been good enough for a professional career. It was also at Carman United that Metcalf acquired the deep religious convictions and the Methodist-derived commitments to hard work, thrift and self-denial that would so animate his working life. By 1922, he had helped form a young man's Bible class, somewhat incongruously called The Hustlers, that would prove to be his principal interest, beyond family and work, ever after.

Metcalf received some timely assistance as he came to realize these values and to galvanize his own ambitions. One of the young women active in the church was Victoria Waring. Metcalf had noticed her working on the line at Neilson where she spent her days nestling chocolates into tiny pleated brown paper cups. At Carman United, where her family was also active, she seemed much more interesting. She was strong-minded and quietly inspiring. She couldn't help but notice her suitor's great potential; she coaxed and pushed him to try to realize it. At her urging, Metcalf began to take night courses in mathematics and accounting. Later she made him choose between romance with her and boxing, and he wisely chose the former. By 1926 they were married and George had moved from the stockroom into the front office. A few rapid promotions later, he was in the sales department.

Selling was truly his métier and the late 1920s was a great time to be a salesman. With the economy booming, the sweet tooths of Toronto were more insatiable than ever and the young Metcalf hustled through the waiting rooms of one food retailer after another. Often he crossed paths with an equally obsessed and buoyantly self-confident bread and biscuit salesman named Garfield Weston. As he twisted the arms of everyone from corner-store operators to emerging food chain owners such as Theodore Loblaw and Milton Cork, he learned, just as Weston was learning, the elementary principles of sales. "When you're a salesman like I am, you act," he said years later. "You make the calls and you keep making them. A man can never be a salesman with anything less than a maximum effort. The sale begins when the customer says 'No.' "He knew whereof he spoke: he had spent two years hounding Cork at Loblaws before he got his first order.

By 1929, as Neilson's newly appointed assistant sales manager, he found himself getting an education in the promotional aspects of business as well. The story goes that Metcalf was critical of the company's major promotional vehicle, a weekly radio show of light classical music called the "Neilson Hour." In one of the few recorded instances of blunt opinion of his career, he passed on his complaints to his boss, sales manager R.P. Smith who invited Metcalf to do better, whereupon he became the show's producer in charge of a budding studio orchestra that included such hopefuls as first violinist Percy Faith.

"My father was always known for his spectacular ability to work," recalls George Metcalf, Jr. "This was the period when he would depart for the office at 7 A.M. and get back about 2 A.M. He would do this five days a week and then go into the office shorter hours on Saturday. And then Sunday would be taken up with the other main thing in his life, the Hustlers Bible class." For a long time though, this unstinting work didn't seem to be getting him anywhere. Whether it was his lack of formal education or simply R.P. Smith's predisposition to stay put, Metcalf didn't make it into the sales manager's office until 1945. And when he did, the promotion was bittersweet. The job marked a tremendous

elevation from his stockroom days and Neilson, with an estimated net worth of $3 million, was by anyone's measure a
significant company. Yet with Morden Neilson, William's son, in
the presidency and assorted other Neilsons waiting in the wings,
further advancement was a distant prospect.

Metcalf's abilities were not going unrecognized outside the
company, however. At Loblaws, where he was now able to sell
Neilson's products with the regularity of the rising sun, president J. Milton Cork and his son Justin were developing a high
regard for his talents. They were aware that Metcalf's calls to
hundreds of stores over the years had given him all kinds of ideas
on ways to boost sales. Likewise, he seemed to them to have fine
instincts about potential store locations. In 1946 the Corks asked
him to join Loblaws, not as a salesman but as a vice-president.
Metcalf was understandably flattered, but he soon found himself
in a quandary. When he informed Morden Neilson of the offer,
Neilson confided to him that he had developed leukemia and was
dying. The future of the family-run company was in doubt. Faced
with this, Metcalf's loyalty came to the fore and he agreed to stay
on as long as Neilson was alive.

By spring of the following year, Neilson had died and Garfield
Weston was in town, offering to buy the control block of shares
in William Neilson Ltd. from the dead man's estate. One of the
people he consulted when deciding to make his offer was his old
fellow traveller in the selling wars, George Metcalf. Weston, who
was even more acute than the Corks when it came to recognizing
ability, trooped over to the Gladstone Avenue plant and after a
meeting with Metcalf practically insisted that he stay on. Metcalf, however, was now committed to Loblaws and he told
Weston half-jokingly that all he had to do to ensure that they
worked together was to buy Loblaws. Weston was dismayed.
He'd seen enough of Loblaws' financial reports to know that the
company had been suffering from slow-growing sales and stag-
nant earnings. Even making allowances for the disruptions of
war, it simply didn't make sense to Weston that a company in

1947 should still be trying to recapture 1939 levels of profitabil-
ity. Before he'd consider anything, he told Metcalf, he'd have his
accountants give the grocery chain a thorough review. Metcalf
stretched his warmest smile and told him in effect not to bother.
With Loblaws, he said, like the salesman he was, it's the future
that counts.

Despite its sagging bottom line, Loblaw Groceterias Co. was by
the late 1940s nothing less than a Canadian entrepreneurial
success story, a chain of 113 stores with annual sales of more
than $50 million a year and profits that fell in the $1 million
range. The chain had been built from scratch by two rough-and-
tumble but commercially ambitious and intuitive businessmen
with whom Metcalf could easily identify. One was a rural
visionary named Theodore Pringle Loblaw; the other was his
partner, a small city grocery store owner's son, J. Milton Cork.
    Loblaw especially seemed to have emerged triumphant from
the school of hard knocks. Born in Alliston, Ontario, in 1872, he
was less than a year old when his father died. When he was 15,
his mother passed away as well, leaving him to the care of his
grandparents who ran a small farm just outside town. They
promptly halted his brief academic career — he made it part way
through the local high school — and put him to work. As a
middle-aged millionaire grocery store chain operator, he would
spend his weekends on his vast, 18-bedroom farm at Alliston,
reinvigorating himself by working a horse-drawn plough or
"drawing a line behind a team," as he would have put it. During
adolescence though, ploughing the rocky soil of central Ontario
seemed only slightly preferable to a life sentence in prison. In
1889, his pocket filled with the princely sum of $20 that he had
earned working in the fields and picking apples, Loblaw struck
out for Toronto. He soon discovered it wouldn't be easy. With
Christmas fast approaching, the 17-year-old tramped the streets
in search of a job, and finally, at a small King Street East grocery
store owned by William Cork, he found one. For $3 a week, Cork
informed him, Loblaw would be a junior clerk; his son Milton

would show him the ropes. He would have Sunday and two evenings a week off, and fringe benefits would consist of occasional grocery items.

His boyhood dream of becoming a locomotive engineer having now faded from his mind, Loblaw plunged into the grocery trade. On his precious nights off, he took courses in accounting and bookkeeping; he absorbed every aspect of the business, from the ways you present fresh merchandise down to the drudgery of maintaining customers' monthly accounts. One of his first innovations for his employer, in fact, was the introduction of a new, more efficient record-keeping system. Loblaw also learned the virtues of thrift. "The longer I live," he stuffily told an interviewer many years later, "the more I am convinced that the difference between the clerk who saves part of his salary and the one that spends all of his is the difference in a few years between the owner of a business and the man out of a job."

Milton Cork, his day-to-day workmate and now his fast friend, had much the same approach to life, the difference being that while Loblaw was a finance and systems man, Cork seems to have been more the consummate retailer, willing to devote most of his waking hours to getting customers into his store and then encouraging them to buy. He too was a small-town boy, born in 1870 in Picton on the shores of Lake Ontario, and he entered his father's Toronto store at the age of 16. Cork's zeal for work was legendary; well into his seventies he would keep Loblaws' store managers on their toes with his unplanned visits, during which he would quietly but forcefully dispense retailing tips on everything from the need to display canned peaches to the best method for sweeping an aisle: you pulled the broom toward you rather than pushing it away so that you didn't sweep the dirt onto the customer's feet.

By the first decade of this century, both men were experienced businessmen. Loblaw, true to his convictions, had used his savings to buy an interest in a second store owned by William Cork. And within a few years, experience drew Loblaw and Milton Cork to similar conclusions about the future of the grocery business. One was that the system whereby food producers and processors set retail prices, the accepted method prior to the First World War, was thoroughly uncompetitive. If grocers could fix their own prices they could be more competitive; if that led to slimmer profit margins then they could compensate by selling more volume. Consumers would end up saving money on their weekly food bills while, in all probability, the grocers would end up richer. Another realization was that the standard method of serving customers — politely delivering groceries and settling up once a month — was cumbersome, expensive for the store owner and hardly conducive to steady cash flow. Why not have people simply pay for the goods at the time of purchase and take them home immediately — in other words, cash and carry?

In 1919, the two men decided to put their ideas to the test. They formed a partnership and opened the first Loblaws' store at the intersection of Dundas and Keele Streets in the west end of Toronto. They opened their second store the following year and another two stores the year after that. From then on the growth was exponential. By 1930, there were no fewer than 95 Loblaws' stores across Ontario. Sales, which had barely touched the $200,000 mark in 1920, were now $18.4 million; in the same period profits had jumped to $1.1 million from $14,000. In engineering this remarkable performance, both Loblaw and Cork became rich men. The two had reorganized their company, Loblaw Stores Ltd., in 1921 to form Loblaw Croceterias Co. which took over the assets and operations of their partnership. And by 1925, in need of more cash to finance the store expansion program, they took Loblaws public with a $545,000 offering of preferred shares. By 1929, with their equity base expanded considerably thanks to a couple of well-timed stock splits and the frantic buying in the stock market at the time, Loblaw and Cork were wealthy on paper and firmly in charge; between them they controlled 55% of the company's voting shares.

Even the Depression was a harbinger of good fortune for Loblaws because it helped revolutionize the food retailing industry. In 1930, a veteran A & P and Kroger Grocery employee named Michael J. Cullen took over an abandoned garage on the outskirts of Jamaica, New York. His plan, considered terribly risky by the incredulous A & P executives who'd been asked to bankroll it, was to turn the garage into a vast, no-frills store with low overheads that would sell high volumes of national brand merchandise at low markups. Since people had less money to spend on food, he'd simply attract more of them using bold, price-related newspaper advertising. What's more, Cullen planned to add specialized departments to handle everything from meat to dairy products so that customers would have one-stop shopping, and for the increasing number of them who owned automobiles, he'd even give them a free place to park. A & P turned him down flat, but he plunged the savings he'd accumulated over 28 years into the venture; before the year was out he opened King Kullen, "the world's greatest price wrecker." It was the first true supermarket.

King Kullen more vividly dramatized what was happening in the industry through the 1920s and 1930s. Many of the retailing principles on which supermarkets were based had been around for some time. Self-service, for instance, dated from 1916 when the maverick and at times eccentric U.S. retailer Clarence Saunders opened his first Piggly Wiggly Store. (Saunders eventually lost a bundle with Piggly Wiggly but he kept coming back with more outlandish retailing concepts. In the 1940s, for example, he started a chain known as Keedoozle Stores in which sample merchandise was displayed in individual locked cases. The customers were given keys to insert into a lock which in turn activated a buzzer in the stockroom and the selection was then loaded onto a conveyor belt for delivery to the cash register.) Likewise, cash and carry was standard at many chains, and in the U.S. southwest, shoppers already took free parking for granted. Cullen's brilliance was that he managed to put it all together. Though he died prematurely following an appendicitis operation in 1936, his influence on the food retailing business continued to be felt.

At the end of March, 1933, T.P. Loblaw entered Toronto's

Western Hospital for a fairly routine sinus operation. It was late in the week and he was confident enough of an early release that he'd arranged to address the Sunday evening service of Dale Presbyterian Church. Fervent religious commitment had accompanied his increasing business success and in recent years Loblaw had come under the sway of the Oxford Group Movement, which promoted its own brand of evangelical Christianity. He didn't make the engagement. After the operation meningitis set in and within three days, at the age of 61, he was dead. At the funeral in Timothy Eaton Church, Cork and hundreds of other mourners sat in stunned silence as the Reverend J.B. Thomson characterized the dual nature of the deceased tycoon: "Many people here think of Mr. Loblaw as a successful businessman, as a merchant prince," he said. "I cherish the memory of him as a flaming evangelist."

After bequests for his adopted children as well as sums left to the likes of Emmanuel College at the University of Toronto, Loblaw bequeathed the bulk of his stock in Loblaw Groceterias to the Toronto Kiwanis Club with the stipulation that it be used to promote healthy activities for boys. Eventually, shares from the estate were also sold to investment trusts in the United Kingdom. Cork, for his part, held on to his block, which now represented the single largest stake in the company, assumed the presidency and soldiered on.

By any standard he waged a successful campaign. Although rationing and staffing problems plagued the chain through the Second World War, as they did all other businesses that directly related to the war effort, sales generally climbed higher each year, breaking through the $50 million mark in 1947. Earnings, while flat after the late thirties, never dipped below $1 million. And with the economy returning to normal after the war, potential for growth seemed limitless. Consumers were beginning to spend again, a fact eloquently reflected in the rising inflation rate now that wartime price controls had been abolished. People were settling down to life in new homes, buying new cars and adding electrical appliances. They were also having babies in what seemed to be record numbers.

The growing prosperity had not escaped George Metcalf's attention. As he debated Loblaws' potential worth with Weston — which in any event was positively confirmed by the accountants — he may have considered the birth rate, something he later called "the most explosive force ever invented." Weston was convinced, and Milton Cork, now 77 and losing steam, was willing to sell. On August 27, 1947, Weston agreed to buy 111,500 of Cork's Class B Loblaw shares for $3.6 million. The price would be paid over five years and amounted to a slight premium over the stock's highest trading price that year of $31.50. Weston would later transfer the stock to George Weston Ltd. and would go on adding to the Loblaw holdings through George Weston Ltd. until he gained voting control of the company in 1955. In January of the following year, a new holding company, Loblaw Companies Ltd., was created as a George Weston Ltd. subsidiary in order to control the ownership of Loblaw Groceterias and serve as a parent company for any other food retailing acquisitions.

Metcalf quickly established himself as Weston's close ally, most notably in 1952 when he sold a block of 25,000 of his own Class B Loblaw shares to his boss. The deal caused a fury of protest from other shareholders. Metcalf had been sold the shares from the company's treasury in October, 1952 at $25 each, $12 under the prevailing market price, in return for meritorious service. He quickly turned around and sold them to Bansco & Co., a Bank of Nova Scotia nominee company representing Garfield Weston, for $32 each. The market at the time of sale was in the $39-$40 range. At the annual meeting in October, 1953, shareholders threw up one scorching question after another as Justin Cork, Loblaws' president, and Richard Meech, its general counsel, sprang to Metcalf's defence. "Mr. Metcalf is not a wealthy man and he did not have the money to purchase the shares so he sold them to one who was in a position to buy them," Meech argued. "There was no such spread [in price] when the deal was arranged, but the market price of the shares rose in the interval."

This sort of deal would never be allowed to happen in the

infinitely more disclosure-conscious 1980s. At the time, however, it was perfectly legal and, in view of the secretive way in
which both Weston and Metcalf preferred to operate, it was
totally consistent with their usual behaviour. The point that the
angered shareholders seemed to be missing, as Metcalf himself
pointed out to the meeting, was that during his six years with the
company, growth had been extraordinary. As many as 77 supermarkets had been opened and sales had increased roughly
threefold to $176 million a year.

   If anything, this assertion considerably underestimated Metcalf's contribution. After only a year with Loblaws, he was the
company's general manager; by 1954 he was president. Once
George Weston Ltd. had control of the company in 1956, Metcalf
went on a preauthorized corporate buying spree that wouldn't
be equalled until the take-over binge of the late 1970s and early
1980s. In a study prepared for the Royal Commission on Corporate Concentration in 1976, Burns Fry Ltd. research analyst
Donald Tigert estimated that between 1953 and 1975, Loblaw
Groceterias spent $309.5 million on take overs. Making allow-
ance for related asset disposals, the estimated net cost of the
program was $258 million. George Weston Ltd. and Loblaws
became truly international, building up major U.S. chains such as
Loblaw Inc. in western New York and acquiring others such as
the Chicago-based National Tea Co. George Metcalf, Jr., remembers the 1950s as a bewildering round of store openings: "Every
time I turned around, it seemed as if there was another Loblaws'
supermarket going up."

   Among Metcalf's principal targets were family-controlled
food wholesalers. They tended to supply independent food
markets and through the late 1940s and early 1950s, it looked as
if the independents', and hence the wholesalers', markets were
going to be swamped by the rapidly growing supermarket
chains. This was the thinking behind Loblaws' acquisition of
National Grocers Co. Ltd. in 1955 and of Atlantic Wholesalers in
1959. In some cases, Metcalf was the first person to show up on a
more than willing seller's doorstep. Dionne Ltée., a family-

controlled retail chain in Montreal, had thought of approaching Dominion Stores, but Loblaws got there first.

As he hopped across North America by plane or orchestrated buy-outs from his nondescript panelled office near a Loblaws' warehouse on the Toronto waterfront, Metcalf developed an almost patented method of operation. He told as few people as possible what he was doing, his natural secrecy aided by the fact that he kept a very small head office staff (he would later do the same at George Weston Ltd. when he became president and managing director of the parent in 1954). Many of his biggest acquisitions weren't revealed to stockholders in either Loblaws or Westons until 1966 when, under pressure from a parliamentary enquiry into food prices, the company revealed its holdings. Metcalf was also stringent about keeping on the previous owners to manage the companies, a logical decision considering that the increasing scope and diversity of the empire would have made it impossible to continuously add fresh management talent. This prolonged relationship with sellers was true of buy-outs ranging from the western retailing chain, Kelly Douglas & Co., to Atlantic Wholesalers.

As much as possible, Metcalf also maintained a laissez-faire management style with his subordinates. Heads of companies whose sales and earnings increased from year to year at least in line with competitors' were ignored. Those whose performance was lacking were summoned to Metcalf's office in Toronto where they immediately noticed that the "Finish Right" sign had been replaced with an even less subtle slogan which read "A Sense of Urgency."

While shareholders might have appreciated and sympathized with Metcalf's zeal for character building, perhaps best exemplified in his later years by his friendship with the doyen of positive thinking, Dr. Norman Vincent Peale, his secretiveness ultimately became frustrating. At the 1964 Loblaws' annual meeting, for instance, one shareholder asked if the company's profit margins and overall efficiency had improved. Metcalf merely smiled benignly and said, "That is a very technical question. It would be difficult to answer." On another occasion, when pressed on diversification plans, he invoked religion to slide away from a direct response. "The Good Book," he said, "holds that we must be meek as a lamb and shrewd as an adder."

No doubt he truly believed that the slightest piece of inside information could give aid and comfort to competitors, but he did carry his paranoia to extremes. "I went to his office one day with a ton of questions on strategic issues," recalls Don Tigert. "He said he would answer all of them, that he'd phone Buffalo and Chicago. He sat there for hours reminiscing. I went there at 2 P.M. and left at 6 P.M. He poured me about ten cups of their Pride of Arabia tea; then he sent me home with a little gift pack of all their products. He dispatched me, but I never learned a damn thing." The same could often be said of executives in Loblaw subsidiaries. At the George Weston Ltd. head office in the old Bank of Commerce building on King Street, Metcalf shrewdly maintained two waiting rooms so that visiting executives from group companies wouldn't see familiar faces and realize they were both serving the same master.

In the end, it wasn't Metcalf's furtive nature that would be held against him. Nor was it his acquisitiveness, given the fact that his companies tended regularly to generate the large amounts of cash that made further take overs possible. (Failing that, Metcalf and Weston were always adept at doing intricate purchases involving shares and other considerations, or at swapping assets from one holding company to another, in ways that left the overall financial underpinnings firm.) The real problem, eventually, was that the empire was getting too big to handle and that significant parts of it were under-performing. The most damaging criticism ever levelled at Metcalf appeared in Tigert's 1976 Royal Commission study, where he noted that sales levels in both retailing and wholesaling companies in the Loblaw group from the early 1950s to the mid-1970s had been below average and that profit margins in the retail companies were "far below average." That this was true was irrefutable; by the late 1960s, other studies were noting that the typical Loblaw subsidiary was earning about 1.4% on sales, only about half the amount that Weston subsidiaries in Europe and Australia were making. Metcalf had been the chief designer in the building of a corporate Frankenstein, and while the monster was in no danger of collapse, many of its limbs were diseased. Metcalf, however, would not be the man to effect the cure. That would be up to a new generation of managers, one of whom was the boss's son.

CHAPTER 6

Life at the Top

> *"It's just that Fortnum's has always been so*
> *completely British."*
>
> Anonymous well-to-do lady shopper,
> London, 1951

Garfield Weston's first official act as controlling stockholder of Fortnum & Mason Ltd. was to give all his employees raises. Executives and managers of the luxury grocer got 10% increases while lower-ranking staff members received 5%. Weston also took pains to reassure the other stockholders that he wasn't some arch philistine from the colonies bent on throwing more than two centuries of quaint retailing tradition on the scrap heap. As he had noted at the pivotal May 4, 1951, shareholders' meeting at London's Caxton Hall where control of the firm had been decided, "Fortnum & Mason should not be kicked around as a public football. As long as I live, these shares will never leave my hands, and I will see that the company is not used as a public football." About a week later, he again spoke of his ownership of Fortnum's, this time with an earnestness that Dr. Arnold might have employed when talking of his young charges at Rugby School. "I am fully conscious of my responsibility to the public and to the store," he said. "I am most impressed with the spirit of the organization; its executive is second to none in business, I will continue with great pride what has rightly been called a great British institution."

At no time, however, did he say that he wouldn't try to refine operations of the institution. By 1957, when the store discreetly marked its 250th anniversary with the introduction of 250 Fino sherry and a new Celebration brand tea blend, Weston had made several major changes. Among the first things that had made his dowager customers blanch was the introduction of cash registers, although he had the good taste to make sure they had no vulgar bells to announce sales. Weston's motive was a practical one. Fortnum & Mason was largely an account business when he acquired control and he wanted to expand the clientele by moving to a cash basis. At the same time, he wanted to give his customers more things to buy, so he broadened the store's product lines to include men's and women's clothing, small appliances and new departments specializing in antiques, gifts and leather goods as well as the traditional delights for the champagne and picnic hamper set. To finish things off, he opened a soda fountain (where you could get such un-North American snack items as game pie and watercress sandwiches with your ice cream soda), and a hair-dressing salon with dryers that purred discreetly rather than whining metallically like those in more plebeian salons. Eventually he would erect a large decorative clock above the store's main entrance on Piccadilly, featuring four-foot-high metal figures of the founders, candle merchant William Fortnum and Queen's footman Hugh Mason, that emerged from behind bronze doors on the hour to bow mechanically to one another. The payoff for these expenditures was that old customers kept on coming, even if they trembled occasionally at the prospect of change, and new ones were added; a reasonable, if not spectacular, increase in profits was the result. From 1950, the year before Weston's purchase of control, to 1964, net income rose from $377,800 to $583,794.

The growth and change at Fortnum's could be taken as a metaphor, albeit an understated one, for the spectacular expansion of Garfield Weston's overall holdings that took place in the decade and a half after 1951. Rather than sitting back and basking in his role as one of Britain's premier industrialists, he in fact seemed more restless and driven than ever and ready to acquire in all directions. While the guidance of his affairs in the United States and Canada could increasingly be ceded to George Metcalf and other top managers, he roamed the rest of the developed world, gradually assembling corporate groups that could rightly be considered empires on their own. Initially in Britain, then in continental Europe, Australia, New Zealand and South Africa, he brought together a sprawling network that, by 1966, had assets of roughly $360 million and annual sales of slightly more than $3 billion. To put these figures in perspective, there were only two other food companies in the world, Unilever in the United Kingdom and A & P in the United States, whose annual sales exceeded Weston's worldwide totals by the mid-1960s. (In Unilever's case, it's also fair to point out that a good part of its size was attributable to other non-food activities including chemicals, tobacco and manufacturing.) Even more impressive is the fact that at the time, Weston's holdings were considered the largest in the world under one person's control. The man who had once said that he dealt "in bread and dreams" had certainly not lost any of his capacity to turn fantasy into reality.

In building this leviathan, Weston didn't lose sight of the operating principles that had served him well earlier in his career. He still went after the best management talent he could find; now he was working on second- and third-generation executives in some of his companies' top jobs. Although it was becoming physically more difficult because of the time and distances involved, he endeavoured to keep in touch with the grass roots, travelling relentlessly from the wood-panelled confines of his home base office at Fortnum & Mason. Looking back from the vantage point of the 1980s, you could argue that Weston was pioneering some of the strategies that management theorists Thomas J. Peters and Robert Waterman, Jr., would later glorify in their bestselling *In Search of Excellence*. Weston always projected a sense of corporate values and culture, if only because his personal values — hard work, religion and the preservation of the Empire — infused his companies. More importantly, as he soared through the booming economic cycle of the 1950s in Britain and elsewhere, he generally remembered to stick with the things he knew best — food processing and retailing.

Weston's vehicle for most of his corporate expansion outside North America was Allied Bakeries, the outgrowth of the original British holding company Weston formed in 1935, Food Investments Ltd. (Fortnum's was a rare exception, held through a personal U.K. investment company, George Weston Holdings Ltd.) Allied, which would later be renamed Associated British Foods Ltd., was used mostly to buy up assorted small bakeries and flour mills through the early 1950s. By 1955 Allied was considered Britain's largest bakery conglomerate and was responsible for roughly 10% of all bread sales in the United Kingdom. That year, however, Allied made its first significant diversification beyond food processing and retailing by offering slightly more than $8.7 million to buy control of the Aerated Bread Co. Ltd. Despite its name, Aerated Bread was best known for its chain of 164 low-budget self-service tea rooms or ABC shops. Suddenly, Weston was the owner of Britain's second largest low-end restaurant-chain operator, after the Joe Lyons Corner House chain. Allied's next major moves came four years later when it acquired 80% of the shares in Food Securities Ltd. of London, a food wholesaler and distributor, and all the shares of Cooper and Co. Stores Ltd., a small retail grocery chain with outlets in England and Scotland. Two years later, in 1961, Allied again took to the acquisition trail, buying up all of Vitbe Flour Mills through another holding company, as well as purchasing a major London bakery chain, A.B. Hemmings Ltd.

To give some idea of the pace at which Weston acquired companies, it has to be remembered that these purchases represent only the high points of Allied's activity over a six-year period. What's more, they don't touch on the momentous decision Garfield Weston took sometime around 1961 to transform Britain's high streets with supermarkets. Weston had already incorporated a new subsidiary at Associated British Foods, Fine Fare (Holdings) Ltd., and that fall he announced that his newest creation planned to spend more than $80 million over the next few years to open literally hundreds of new stores.

It wasn't hard to see why he felt this seemingly flamboyant investment would yield vast rewards. The North American chains owned by George Weston Ltd., notably Loblaw Groceterias Co. in Ontario and National Tea Co. in the U.S. midwest, had participated in what could only be described as the explosive growth of the supermarket business in the 1950s. The baby boom, rising incomes and massive population shifts from cities to suburbs all fuelled the change in shopping habits, pushing the supermarkets' share of all U.S. food sales from 35% in 1950 to 70% in 1960. At peak construction in the early part of the decade, three supermarkets a day were opening up somewhere in Canada or the United States. Supermarkets were no longer oddities; they had become a focal point of North American culture.

Supermarket development on this scale had not yet occurred in the United Kingdom, but there were signs that it was possible. Britain in the late 1950s and early 1960s was in its "I'm all right, Jack" era. Conservative Prime Minister Harold Macmillan was ensconced at 10 Downing Street and the country was relatively affluent. Business volumes and incomes were growing at reasonable levels, and employment was high. And if there were occasional signals that the nation's trade balance was starting to deteriorate, it wasn't anything that couldn't be righted with a bit of effort. Emerging supermarket retailers like Sainsburys and Tesco could see that British shoppers were different from middle Americans — for one thing, the English tended to shop daily rather than weekly like their Yankee cousins — but then they could adapt the formula to suit the market. The average super-market size in Britain was 10,000 square feet or less instead of the American standard of 20,000 square feet or more, a reflect-ion of the fact that older built-up areas in the United Kingdom simply didn't have the vast sites available in the limitless suburbs of America. Over time this would change, of course. Urban renewal and new town development made larger sites available, complete with American-style parking lots to accommodate the growing ranks of Austin Minis and Ford Anglias that were appearing on British roads. In the four years between 1957 and 1961, the number of supermarkets (defined in this case as stores with selling areas of at least 2,000 square feet) in the United Kingdom jumped from 80 to 600 and more were on the way. As one chain operator described it, retailers were about to "do for the food shopper what Marks and Spencer has done for the clothes shopper."

Weston wanted his share of any development and he indicated as much with an appropriately dramatic gesture. As part and parcel of Fine Fare's store opening program, he announced a plan to import as many as 2,000 young Canadian men between the ages of 18 and 25 initially to work in, and eventually to manage, his new stores. Canadians were necessary, he said, because whereas supermarkets were alien enterprises to the British, there wasn't a Canadian lad over the age of 12 who hadn't either worked in one or shopped in one enough to understand how it worked. Over the course of their two-year hitches, the members of this commando team, as Weston likened them, would instil this understanding in their British co-workers. Weston's an-nouncement was also tinged with his old Empire refrain. The presence of all these young Canadians, he added, would remind the British, now eagerly pushing for membership in the Euro-pean Common Market, of their traditional Commonwealth ties.

The first 500 would be recruited in Canada beginning in the fall of 1961 and, indeed, that October, Weston staged a massive farewell dinner at Toronto's Royal York Hotel for the initial 50 recruits. On hand for this paramilitary occasion was none other than Field Marshal Viscount Montgomery, who was passing through town on his way home to Britain from China. With his classic cold stare, Montgomery looked down from the head table as Weston did a close inspection of the ranks of his clerks' regiment, giving them last-minute handshakes and words of encouragement.

Expansion across the English Channel was a little more measured, if only because Weston had to gradually bring his Empire and Commonwealth convictions into line with the new economic realities. By 1962, Weston was publicly disparaging the British move to join the European Economic Community. At a luncheon in May, arranged for Commonwealth newspaper correspondents by his old guru and Empire booster Lord Beaverbrook, Weston heatedly told journalists that "we're standing on the edge of an abyss," that Britain's swing toward Europe was an act of economic desperation that could be counteracted only by a concerted drive by the advanced Commonwealth countries to set up a separate trading bloc. Reaction in the Dominion of Canada at least was highly negative. Editorialists suggested that Weston and Beaverbrook were living in the past, given that Canadian trade with Britain and Commonwealth trading preferences had long been a declining factor in Canada's balance of trade picture. The *Globe and Mail* also expressed surprise at Weston's views, given the fact that he'd just presided over Associated British Foods' purchase of a 45% stake in West Germany's largest supermarket chain, Deutscher Supermarkt Handels-GmbH. Earlier that year Weston, with his typical gusto, had won official West German blessing for the investment by convincing Chancellor Ludwig Erhard in a private audience that he was the man who could make sure that food retailing would share in West Germany's economic miracle.

Early the following year, Weston had overcome his old Empire loyalties sufficiently that he invested in France, although in this case the eventual purchase of a 94% share in the grocery chain Entrepôts Dubuffet was shrouded in intrigue worthy of a spy novel. Late in 1962, Weston told the Associated British Foods annual meeting that the company was planning to expand in France with the blessing of President Charles de Gaulle. The rumoured take-over target was Savoir Economiser, or Saveco, a small but rapidly growing discount chain. French government officials denied that their president had formed what the London dailies were calling "a Grand Alliance" between himself and Weston under which harsh French rules preventing the take-over of domestic companies by foreign firms were being temporarily suspended. Weston, twisting practicalities to suit ideology, noted that his pending deal with the French was a good example of the way Britain should behave in its international economic dealings. De Gaulle, he said, was concerned about holding down food prices and had come to Weston because he was a strong retailer. If Britain developed her Commonwealth ties, she too could negotiate with Europe from strength and need not join the Community. Treaties such as the one that formed the Common Market were for "weak countries, not strong countries," he said. In Britain's case, the counsellors of doom were the financial men of the City of London who, in Weston's estimation, were willing to sacrifice the nation on the altar of Europe in order to achieve their own nefarious ambitions to become the underwriters and moneychangers of the Continent. (Weston's pro-Commonwealth stance later became somewhat more frenzied when he predicted such dire consequences as the end of Britain's monarchy — and her merchant marine — should she pursue Common Market membership. His arguments even took on a Canadian nationalist tone when he complained to journalists that the United States was encouraging Britain to join Europe because it would then be easier for the Americans to swallow up Canada.)

His overreaction notwithstanding, Weston was acting as a role model for Britain by developing what seemed to be the corporate equivalent of a Commonwealth trading bloc. Beginning in the early 1950s, Weston had picked up interests in Australia and New Zealand, initially through a local subsidiary, Weston Biscuit Co. In 1954 he dispatched his second eldest son, Garry, to Australia as its managing director. The younger Weston had already completed degrees at Oxford and Harvard and was working on a law degree at McGill when he headed for Sydney. Now he turned his energies to expanding his father's Australasian holdings. In 1962, with his father's guidance, he incorporated a new holding company to oversee Australian operations, George Weston Foods Ltd. Later that year, the new company bought N.B. Love Industries Ltd., a New South Wales animal feed, flour and starch producer, and the following year it bought a large baker and miller, W. Thomas Industries Proprietary Ltd. By 1965, along with assorted other purchases, George Weston Foods owned no fewer that 33 bakeries, 11 flour mills and 10 factories that made everything from glucose to bedding and furniture. In the key urban centres of Australia's most heavily populated region, New South Wales, including the cities of Sydney, Canberra and Newcastle, it was estimated that Weston-owned bakeries had roughly one-third of the market.

As Garfield Weston told Associated British Foods shareholders, one of the main reasons he had been attracted to Australia and New Zealand had been the favourable commercial attitudes of governments in both countries. "They permit a high level of self-investment and there is a welcome absence of onerous restrictions on the exercise of business initiative." This was precisely why he found South Africa appealing as well. In 1963, Associated British Foods bought a 51% controlling interest in the Premier Milling Co. Ltd. of Johannesburg for about $15 million. Premier would always be regarded skeptically by outsiders, a significant but contained investment in what was becoming by the day a more and more repressive country. In North America, except to the minority of politically minded people who were willing to wade through Associated British Foods' annual reports for details and snippets of information, the Premier investment seemed no more noteworthy than the purchase of a big flour mill. However, Premier was in fact a sizable conglomerate all on its own. Under Weston's acquisitive influence, it quickly used internally generated cash and equity and debt borrowings to add to its own holdings in fields ranging from bakeries and edible oil processing to gift shops and pharmaceuticals. By the mid-1960s, the South African *Financial Mail* listed Premier as South Africa's seventh largest public industrial company; in the baking and milling industries it was far and away the republic's largest. Sales by this time had risen to more than $200 million a year while profits were more than $10 million, enough to make a happy difference to Associated British Foods' bottom line.

With the growing size of Weston's interests around the world, there inevitably came increased corporate complexity. Holding companies and operating subsidiaries were set up for special purposes, whether to provide for overall family control (as was the case with Wittington Investments Ltd. in North America and George Weston Holdings in the United Kingdom), to deal with specialized functions such as real estate services for retail arms such as Loblaws or Fine Fare, or to provide company bridges between far-flung outposts of the empire. The labyrinthine corporate structure was deliberate. Until Weston was forced by public pressure to disclose the extent of his holdings in 1966, he enjoyed a comforting privacy that allowed top managers to do and undo deals that today would quite often require shareholder approval. Another benefit was financial flexibility, the capacity to move money and holdings around and strike deals between subsidiaries that were mutually beneficial, especially when markets were tough.

In mid-May, 1963, Garfield Weston stunned British financial markets in general, and the real estate industry in particular, by announcing that Fine Fare was putting an abrupt halt to its massive building program. The store network, which had been expanding like a huge spider's web across the land, would have to stop for a time because, the Canuck commando clerks notwithstanding, there simply wasn't enough management talent around to staff it. Given the similar strains that others in the industry were facing, it was a plausible explanation. But it wasn't a full one. The speed with which the expansion program had been carried out meant that the store sites selected were often the wrong ones to generate supermarket-scale traffic. Competitors also suggested that Fine Fare's merchandising wasn't up to scratch and that when other retailers took over one of its sites, turnover generally picked up sharply. Even Fine Fare's image was called into doubt. Analysts pointed out that the high end of food retailing had the likes of Sainsbury's while the low end was dominated by chains such as Victor Value and Pricerite. Fine Fare was somewhere in the middle and was not exerting a strong pull on any customer group. These criticisms seemed to be borne out that fall when Fine Fare announced a net loss of $3.7 million for the year ended March 30, 1963.

By the time these figures had been made public, however, Weston had begun to orchestrate an intricate, cross-corporate financial rescue effort. Technically, control of Fine Fare was held by Associated British Foods' subsidiary Howardsgate Holdings Ltd. That June, Howardsgate sold a 51% stake in Fine Fare to Dicoa Ltd. (an acronym for Diversified Companies of America), a previously obscure holding subsidiary of Weston's principal Canadian investment holding company, Wittington Investments Ltd. Dicoa would pay Howardsgate $11.4 million and advance another $17 million to help pay down some of Fine Fare's outstanding loans. Under the deal too, Canadian management would be imported to help revive Fine Fare, including George Metcalf, the Loblaws' president who was now to become chairman of a Dicoa-controlled Howardsgate. As a sideline provision, George Weston Ltd. in Toronto was given an option to buy 100% of Dicoa from Wittington.

The immediate advantages of this Byzantine manoeuvring were that cash was injected into the Fine Fare chain and that its poor fiscal performance in 1963 was neatly excised from Associated British Foods' consolidated income statement, thus preventing any ugly erosion of the parent's profits. If retail analysts wanted to speculate that the deal was primarily to inject some good old Canadian retail management moxie into an under-performing chain, so much the better. Eventually, in late 1966, George Weston Ltd. issued Class A treasury shares and used the proceeds to pick up ownership of Dicoa. George Weston Ltd. also assumed responsibility for outstanding Dicoa debts totalling $18.7 million, a reflection of the money that had earlier been used to help whittle down Fine Fare's debts. This meant that Dicoa's, and hence Fine Fare's, results could be consolidated in George Weston Ltd.'s statement for 1966 and, considering that Fine Fare was now back in the black, the move was a smart one. After making allowances for Dicoa's interest expenses, the bottom line at George Weston Ltd. that year was swollen by $1.34 million.

Despite the financial virtuosity, the situation didn't immediately improve at Fine Fare's 315-odd stores. In the fall of 1963, under Metcalf's influence, the chain began a brief and unpleasant dalliance with trading stamps, an innovation adapted from Loblaws in Canada. Only two weeks previously, stamps had come to Britain courtesy of a smaller chain, Pricerite, and once Fine Fare decided to go along, the reaction was swift. Within two weeks, arch-rival Lord Sainsbury had organized other chains representing some 37,000 grocery shops into an anti-stamp alliance. Sainsbury's also set up a retailers' boycott of Weston's top-selling Sunblest bread. Fine Fare soon dropped the stamps.

Over the next two years Fine Fare considered a number of solutions to its competitive problems. One was to turn some outlets into discount stores; another was simply to sell them or to close them down. By 1965, top management had concluded that roughly one in ten outlets was uneconomic and would need to be remodelled and reopened under new trading names in order to build volume. The strain was taking its toll on top executives, many of whom decided to bail out that summer. Ironically, one who left at that time was Fine Fare managing director Ben Shelley, a Canadian import who had planned to use his North American skills to effect the turnaround.

The departures of Shelley and his colleagues were soon forgotten, thanks to the arrival of James Gulliver. Gulliver, hired by Weston that fall, was a certifiable whiz kid. A Harvard MBA who had already racked up a chain of successes at management consultants Urwick, Orr & Partners Ltd., he was a firm believer in the prevailing boardroom science of the day, management by objectives. Simply put, MBO, as it is called, requires performance targets, short-, medium- and long-term, to be set for all people in all divisions of a company and these are regularly reviewed. In Fine Fare's case, this strategy seemed to make abundant sense. Financial planning was weak, overhead costs seemed to be heading out of control, marketing had been neglected and even warehouse procedures were problem-ridden. Gulliver systematically began developing plans for all these areas. He broke the chain up into four regional groups, each with its own board of directors and unique development policy, and he put greater emphasis on the development of in-house brands in order to foster customer loyalty. Finally, he revised operating methods for everything from shelf-stocking to warehouse shipping. By the time Gulliver was made chairman of Fine Fare (Holdings) in 1967, the good habits had taken root, and when he left the organization in 1972 it was solidly profitable.

Through the 1950s and 1960s, the public perception of Garfield Weston increasingly was one of an aloof, headstrong and highly paternalistic industrialist. Likewise, many people, and especially those on the political left, were inclined to criticize him simply because of who he was; in the 1960s, as the profit motive came into disrepute among the counterculture, it seemed inevitable that one of the world's great profit-makers would take a lot of flak. Judging by his periodic statements, Weston was well aware of such shifts in the public mood and they didn't please him. The sub-text of many of his best-reported speeches, notably the ones he made each spring at the George Weston Ltd. annual meetings in Toronto's Royal York Hotel, was that the old values — loyalty, ideals, hard work — should be strengthened rather than abandoned. Usually after he'd cajoled, lectured and charmingly stroked the phalanxes of perfumed widows and dour retirees who seemed to constitute the majority of George Weston Ltd.'s minority stockholders, he would remind them of his own shining example.

In Weston's mind, there was no distinction between the attitudes and habits he brought to the boardroom and those he applied to life in general. His business values were his personal values. Similarly, the methods he used to promote his business development worked to the public advantage. His idea of importing young Canadian grocery clerks to spearhead Fine Fare's growth was nothing more than a revised and updated version of the exchange program for young men and women he had sponsored in the late 1940s and early 1950s. These visits, involving up to 50 hand-picked young men or women from Britain and Canada, were tightly organized, well-chaperoned, and highly promoted affairs. The youthful participants were given the kind of blanket media coverage accorded royal tours and an eager public was treated to stories about everything from the outfits they wore for presentation to the Queen to what kind of marks they got in school. These young people represented the future of the Commonwealth, and their understanding of the ties between Canada and the Mother Country was crucial. Weston outdid himself in 1953 when he sent 50 young Canadian women on a month-long trip to Britain and France, highlighted by a trip to London in time for the coronation of Queen Elizabeth. Weston also shipped over many of his top Canadian executives and their wives for the coronation. To enable them and the visiting youngsters to watch the regal procession on the big day he built his own bleacher on Oxford Street, complete with outdoor toilets and attendants.

Weston was capable of even more provocative and occasionally offbeat ventures. In 1960, he opened a remote luxury resort called Frenchman's Cove in Jamaica, with his eldest son Grainger as on-site manager. Frenchman's Cove put people up in individual copper-roofed, limestone guest houses, each with a spectacular and uniquely private view of the Caribbean. No cars were allowed on the grounds, nor was there any noisy nighttime entertainment. The well-heeled guests, who paid the then tremendous sum of $2,500 for a two-week visit, could ask to be ferried by car or by private plane to play golf or to sightsee, but most contented themselves with the offerings of the chef, who was imported from Fortnum's, and with the resort's pristine solitude. Frenchman's Cove may in part have been an effort to keep eldest son Grainger, then in his late thirties, involved in the family businesses. (Grainger had been sent to Texas to oversee biscuit operations, but his interest in the empire was minimal. By 1967, Garfield Weston bought a 7,500-ton cruise ship, the *Jamaica Queen*, for $6.4 million. The idea, which was only briefly put into effect, was to have Grainger manage the ship's year-round service between Miami and Jamaica.)

Frenchman's Cove enjoyed a temporary popularity, catering to royalty and the Rockefellers, and to artistic lights such as Picasso and Dylan Thomas. In 1960, it gained a brief notoriety when an employee made the mistake of turning away a car occupied by Hugh Gaitskell, the leader of Britain's Labour Party. But when Jamaican tourism waned in the 1970s, so did the resort's fortunes, and by the time the industry revived, a younger crowd was looking for livelier holiday spots with cheaper packages. By the time a hurricane battered part of the resort in 1980, Grainger was spending most of his time back in San Antonio, Texas, running a regional biscuit concern. (In recent years, Grainger's son, Gregg, has been working to revive the resort, this time trying to sell it to the upper-middle-class rather than to the super-rich.)

Garfield Weston's negative public image was not helped by some dramatic public utterances he made in favour of highly unpopular causes. At the George Weston Ltd. annual meeting in 1964 he lapsed into a defence of South Africa's policy of apartheid. With every word, he got into deeper and deeper trouble as he argued that blacks weren't ready for the vote, that they had no intrinsic right to a share in government power and that, in any event, the government was taking pretty good care of their needs. "And believe me, every black piccaninny or black mammy can fall on the government for solution to any social problem," he declared. Weston, in fact, didn't mean to say that blacks in South Africa should never progress or gain the vote, but any niceties to his position were immediately lost in the withering blast of criticism that followed. African students in Toronto announced plans to picket Loblaws' stores, letters to newspaper editors came fast and furious and the *Toronto Star* excoriated him for his "Uncle Tomish language." Weston made other, less damaging comments. At one meeting, he joked about British Prime Minister Edward Heath's predilection for going sailing with young women. At another, he put himself out of step with just about every politically aware person under the age of 30 by saying he supported the U.S. invasion of Cambodia. (By the late 1960s, Weston had come full circle in his views on the United States. It was no longer an economic juggernaut bent on annexing the Dominion, but rather a protective umbrella in the nuclear age, a country whose aims and objectives Canada should almost automatically support.)

Just to be fair, Weston's extra-business life didn't consist purely of being a political neanderthal. He was, for instance, a notable philanthropist, both on his own and through his charitable foundation. Weston, who maintained that the ability to give money away thoughtfully was considerably harder than earning it in the first place, managed to donate phenomenal sums over the years, for everything from medical research at the University of Toronto to paintings for the McMichael Canadian Collection and the purchase of an eighteenth-century furniture collection for the Royal Ontario Museum.

Weston's intense sense of privacy made it hard for observers to understand his thoughts and motives in his later years. What emerges from the hodge-podge of stories about him in the 1960s is a picture of a restless and somehow unfulfilled man who kept buying companies and moving house because he couldn't bear the thought of keeping still. Hobbies, like raising racehorses, and family occasions — notably a succession of clan gatherings for the invariably lush weddings of his children — were only momentary distractions from the essence of his life — the thrill of closing a deal. He never broadcast his private emotions. When his wife, Reta Howard Weston, died in 1967, her passing, after a marriage of 46 years during which she was probably the greatest prop of Weston's extraordinary career, barely drew public notice.

In 1967, the Dicoa financial assistance plan for Associated British Foods' Fine Fare chain began to come full circle. George Weston Ltd. sold 31% of Fine Fare back to Associated British Foods (ABF) for $23.4 million and, a year later, it sold back the remaining 20% it held for $16.8 million. And just as in 1963, there were valid reasons for reversing the deal. The British pound was strong relative to the Canadian dollar, which meant that the British company could regain control less expensively than it could have previously. In any event, renewed control by ABF was only appropriate, given that it was its management effort rather than that of the Canadian company that had turned the chain around. And as Weston couldn't help but notice, George Weston Ltd. could use the money. Its principal subsidiary, Loblaw Companies, was suffering from declining profits. The George Weston/ Loblaw organization may have been gigantic, but within its multi-faceted empire real problems were brewing.

CHAPTER 7

Lifting the Veil

"It's an astonishing revelation, the enormity of which surprised even the sophisticated."

Response of the Senate and House of Commons
Special Joint Committee investigating food prices to
material supplied by the Weston organization on the
extent of its corporate holdings, December 20, 1966

As the poet T.S. Eliot observed about the end of the world, sometimes great events lack a suitably noisy accompaniment. So it was that the unveiling of Garfield Weston's vast corporate empire took place by degrees, starting in the restrained and at times excessively formal atmosphere of an Ottawa committee hearing room. The exposure happened almost coincidentally, the result of an inquiry that was more concerned about the price of a square meal than about the issue of corporate concentration. It was a bit like digging for potatoes in the backyard garden and coming across a perfectly preserved mastodon.

Through 1965 and 1966, the rate of inflation generally, and for food in particular, became a hot political issue. The economy was growing at what seems in retrospect to have been a phenomenal rate, averaging real annual gains in output of 5.6% through the decade. Primary manufacturing and resource industries were enjoying one of their greatest eras of expansion. Whole new industries seemed to be developing overnight; high-technology firms started sprouting in hitherto commercial backwaters such as Ottawa, and a new breed of entrepreneur, the real estate developer, systematically began to reshape the skylines of Canada's major cities. Stock market investors hadn't had so much fun or been so involved since the penny mining stock booms of earlier decades. The country was about to celebrate its one hundredth birthday, and it was rich.

Canada's prosperity wasn't unique. With the possible exception of Great Britain, all industrialized countries made considerable gains in the sixties. Encouraged by the heated example of the Japanese economy, which was hitting a postwar growth peak of more than 10% a year in real terms, academics, government officials and business people readily concluded that the sky was the limit. But the price of growth was a high rate of inflation. Although the rates experienced in the sixties appear ludicrously low when compared with the double-digit levels of the late seventies, the increasing cost of prosperity rankled, in part because Canadians came to suspect that it had less to do with the cost of imported goods and services or with the rising expense of producing goods at home than it did with the tendency of large corporations to take advantage of buoyant markets to pad their markups. The fact that Canadian prices were visibly higher than those in the United States only made people more suspicious.

Food prices in particular had always been contentious. In 1958, the Conservative government of John Diefenbaker had gone as far as establishing a Royal Commission on Price Spreads of Food Products to investigate the possibility that the emerging supermarket chains were creaming a bit too much off the top. Now, in the mid-1960s, amidst a blizzard of grocery store trading stamps, consumers faced all kinds of promotions disguised as games and lotteries, as well as inconsistent and often puzzling methods of product pricing that made the major chains even more suspect. The relative uniformity of pricing for many nationally advertised brands from one supermarket to the next led many to conclude that the chains might be price fixing. The Liberal government of Lester Pearson knew it had to do something or it could have a consumer revolt on its hands.

This time the government ruled out an expensive and time-consuming royal commission. In the early fall of 1966, it decided instead to expand the terms of reference of a special joint committee of the House of Commons and Senate that was already investigating another area of high public sensitivity, consumer credit. Co-chaired by progressive Liberal Senator David Croll, a veteran provincial and federal politician from Toronto who supported such causes of the left as trade union-ism, and Ron Basford, a young Liberal MP from Vancouver who looked like cabinet material, the committee was populated by workhorses and skeptics — notably New Democrat MP Max Saltsman — who relished the thought of grilling food industry executives. And grill they did. Between September 28 and December 13 of that year, the committee met as many as 42 times and heard briefs and testimony from everybody who was anybody in the food business.

On the morning of Thursday, October 20, it was Loblaw Groceterias Co.'s turn and a delegation of ten executives from the company showed up for the hearing. They were not, however, led by either Garfield Weston or George Metcalf. Both men were hundreds of miles away and not likely to volunteer an appearance. Instead, the spokesman was Richard G. Meech, Loblaw Groceterias' vice-president, secretary-treasurer and longtime corporate counsel. He kicked off the session by guiding the MPs, senators and assorted committee legal counsel through the company's extensive brief. Meech's rendering was part advertisement, part apologia, reasonably informative (although statistics were not always given sufficient context) and occasion-ally condescending. Early on he begged the committee's pardon because copies of the brief were not yet available in French, although he impressed upon them that he was no narrow anglophile. "I want to assure you, honourable senators and gentlemen, that my family and grandchildren are not overlooking the cultural aspects of the French language," he said. "I have seen to that." Later, under questioning, he suggested that any housewife who was complaining about prices should remember the blessings that had been bestowed upon her by the supermarket chains. "The chain-store supermarket has done an awful lot for her in establishing cleanliness in stores, establishing quick distribution of farm products and bringing out a lower rate of prices that did not prevail when there were not such strong groups to do the services which in our type of civilization is demanded," he told the committee. "I think housewives, on reflection, are truly grateful for the service rendered by the chain-store supermarkets."

Meech, at age 73, was still in his prime. With his oval face, his greying hair combed flat to his head, and his slightly hooded eyes magnified by the lenses of his metal-rimmed glasses, he was the quintessential specimen of an earlier, more dignified era in business. Over the roughly 30 years he had put in at Loblaws, he had honed his style to perfection. He radiated stability and sincerity from every pore. He portrayed the supermarket manager as a well-meaning businessman who was stuck between a rock and a hard place. "We are doing our utmost to keep the lid on prices," he told the committee. He tried to enlist his listeners' sympathy for the problems facing chain owners, from demanding labour unions and diseases such as brown rot and soft blight that rendered fresh produce unsalable, to capricious weather patterns that devastated crops and drove up wholesale prices. The supermarket chains were emphatically on the consumers' side, he declared, responding to their needs with everything from house-brand merchandise to national-brand specials. When it was suggested that trading stamps, games and other promotions merely added to store costs, and thus added indirectly to the cost of food products, Meech countered that they were "self-liquidating"; that is, their cost would be paid for not by higher food prices but by a higher volume of sales. In any event, he added, stores used such gimmicks only because consumers wanted them and even needed them to help flesh out their dreary lives. "Have you ever considered how dull it would be for a housewife to go into a store and see nothing but price tickets and a display of produce?" he asked. "It would lose all the romance of life."

There wasn't so much as an ounce of cynicism in this statement. Meech may have been a lawyer by training but he was a grocer at heart and his style and actions spoke volumes about the corporate culture of the Weston group. The son of an English butcher who had emigrated to Canada in 1880, his earliest memories were of delivering orders from his father's Parliament Street shop to the barely developed eastern portions of the city just beyond the Don River. When he spoke of the "wonderful men" he had met in the trade, he was referring to the likes of J. Milton Cork and T.P. Loblaw, the latter of whom had struck a kindly deal with him in the early 1920s. Meech, who had served in the First World War as a machine gunner and later as a pilot with the Royal Flying Corps, was back in Toronto and two years into his law courses at Osgoode Hall when his father died. He dropped out of school to run the shop to provide income for his mother and was toiling away when he received a surprise visit from Loblaw himself. In a lengthy interview with a provincial historian in 1977, Meech recalled their conversation went something like this:

LOBLAW: Young man, I heard that you are studying law and want to be a lawyer.

MEECH: Yes I do, Mr. Loblaw.

LOBLAW: Well, I will buy your father's place. I knew your father well; I will buy his business.

MEECH: I don't know what to ask for it, Mr. Loblaw.

LOBLAW: I'll help you. I want you to take shares.

MEECH: I don't know anything about stock. I'd prefer cash.

LOBLAW: Well, I'll give you cash, but I'm going to give it to you in the form of a mortgage so that you'll have it invested at a good rate of interest for your mother. You can have any excess cash.

MEECH: All right, you're a friend of the family.

LOBLAW: Yes, don't worry about that.

Meech never regretted trading a butcher's apron for a lawyer's robes, but he did have occasion to rue the fact that he didn't initially take Loblaw stock. In 1939, after one of his law partners died and he couldn't agree with the remaining partner on the way to manage the firm, he went to Loblaw Groceterias as legal counsel. After working a short time with Cork and other top officials, he was asked to become vice-president and secretary-treasurer, a post he would hold until 1969 (even today, at 94, he's still listed as an honorary director of Loblaw Companies). Meech was a central player in Loblaw Groceterias', and later Loblaw Companies', phenomenal growth cycles and, as he recalled, "If I had taken Loblaw's advice and taken stock our family would have been very well off."

In any event, Meech didn't do badly, and as a corporate counsel he was nothing short of brilliant when it came to developing and implementing company policy. It was Meech, for example, who handled most of the negotiations as Loblaws was gradually unionized. He had a way of persuading and charming labour officials that took the bite off their demands and generally assured peace in the ranks. As he told it, in fact, it was he who first convinced Milton Cork to accept the idea of unionization, beginning with a group of truck drivers at the company's Fleet Street warehouse in Toronto. Meech went to a meeting with the truck drivers, saw they were being pressured to become part of an American union and wisely told them the company was willing to listen. Then he suggested that they ought to form their own local union. Should they be so inclined, he'd be more than willing to help by drawing up their constitution. Quite aside from the fact that his offer was a smart corporate ploy to disarm a potentially hostile workforce by blanketing it with the company's brotherhood and support, it was also typically paternalistic. That Loblaws' company lawyer should draw up the charter for the Loblaw Truck Drivers' Association was an example of how corporate managers tended to view their employees in the 1940s and 1950s. Meech was even known to call employees with debt problems into his office for fatherly lectures. In some cases, he turned Loblaws into a *de facto* banker, arranging for the company to pay off a long-time employee's debts and have the borrower make one regular consolidated monthly payment to the company. But even at Loblaws, paternalism had its limits. Meech recalled that in the 1950s, inside workers in Sudbury who were members of the Loblaws Store Employees Association wanted maternity leave provisions extended to unmarried mothers. "I was horrified and said that we could never stand for that," Meech recalled. "I said, just imagine the *Sudbury Star* coming out with a banner headline, 'Loblaws subsidizes little bastards.' We wouldn't be in the food business long."

As the hearing trailed through the morning hours, Meech was adamant that it was grossly unfair to suggest that supermarket chains were profiteering at consumers' expense by marking up prices. "The supermarket industry is highly competitive," he told the committee. "Price spreads among the chains are minute. The battle for the consumer's dollar is keen and unrelenting. There is a constant struggle to keep the lid on prices, but rising costs in all sectors of the economy — in business, labour and government — have built up inflationary pressures that are beyond the power of the retailer to control." Yet Meech also aroused the committee's curiosity about the implications that a corporate empire, one with linkages to all levels of the food industry, might have for prices. At one point, the committee wondered what Loblaws' overall labour costs were as a percentage of total sales. "We will supply you with that information," Meech responded, "but I would observe that the company before you today is not a simple company in the food business, such as you have had experience with before. We are a very complex organization. You might say that Loblaws is a holding company with many companies within it, and to break down figures of this nature encompasses quite a bit of accounting."

It wasn't the cost of labour that intrigued committee counsel John J. Urie. At 46, Urie was in the middle of an already long and distinguished career — he'd been called to the Bar at the tender age of 18 — that would be capped by his becoming a federal appeal court judge. He quickly cut through the digressions the committee was taking that morning into the multiple price ticketing of canned fish and the virtues of Proten beef, a popular Swift Canadian Co. line of tenderized meat that was produced by injecting cattle with papaya juice before they were slaughtered. He was interested in finding out why comparable U.S. supermarkets seemed able to prosper with smaller profit margins than their Canadian counterparts:

URIE: Mr. Chairman, I would like to direct a question to Mr. Meech on a little different line. On page four of the brief, Mr. Meech, you state that in Loblaws' retail operations in Canada since 1960 the trend of sales has been upward. In 1961 reported sales were $471 million. What were the sales in 1966 or at the end of your last fiscal year?

MEECH: You have it on the next page, Mr. Urie. It is $613 million.

URIE: I am sorry. Now, your company is made up of a head company and a number of subsidiaries. Do those sales represent the sales of Loblaw Groceterias alone or do they represent your other subsidiaries in Canada as well?

MEECH: They represent other subsidiaries in the retail business.

URIE: Could you tell us what those other subsidiaries are, sir?

MEECH: I will ask Mr. Robertson, our counsel, to answer that question.

ROBERTSON: The consolidated Canadian subsidiaries whose sales are reflected in here include Powers Stores, Pickering Farms, Super City Discount Foods Ltd., Busy Bee and O.K. Economy Stores.

URIE: Do they include Kelly Douglas & Company?

ROBERTSON: They are not a retail operation as I understand it.

(Kelly Douglas at the time was a wholesale food distributor in British Columbia. It didn't develop retailing interests until 1974, when the Loblaw companies were rationalized along geographic lines and retailing interests were transferred from another Loblaw subsidiary, Westfair Foods Ltd.)

URIE: These are only retail sales, and they are not in retail? As I understand it the net profits percentage to sales in 1966 on your $613 million was 1.88%; is that correct?

MEECH: Yes.

URIE: Your company also has a substantial interest in National Tea Co. (of Chicago), or is it wholly-owned?

MEECH: Majority-owned.

URIE: What were the 1966 sales of that company, can you tell us?

R.J. KANE (a Loblaw Groceterias management consultant): The last published sales of National Tea as at December 31, 1965, were $1,158 million, if my memory serves me right.

URIE: What was the net profit percentage to sales of National Tea Co. in the United States? Maybe I can assist you. I have a report here from the *Financial Post* ...

KANE: I was going to say around 1.1 or 1.2.

URIE: The report says .97. Would that be accurate?

KANE: It was about $11.5 million.

URIE: As opposed to 1.8 in Canada. Now other witnesses before us have told us that for Dominion Stores it was 2.07%, Steinbergs 1.9%, and yours is 1.88. Almost all the others were 1% higher than your subsidiary in the United States. Have you any explanation why the percentages vary so greatly between the two countries?

KANE: I am afraid in my capacity I cannot answer that. Maybe somebody in the merchandising field can.

HENRY SHELLY (vice-president and general manager of warehousing): I think the word "volume" must enter into it. Across the border, with their greater population, a smaller percentage is possible.

URIE: The total volume is $500 million higher in the United States. In some cases, some of the other stores that appeared before us were higher or lower than you. Surely it would not account for nearly 1% on net profits? Does that indicate to you that the alleged tremendous competitive market in Canada is not nearly as competitive as it is in the United States? Do you say that prices in the United States are down because of the more stringent competition there?

MEECH: I would think so. I think the competition in the United States is very much keener and forces a lower return all through the various chains. I know they work on a lower margin than Canadian companies.

Urie pressed on with his questions, probing the rate of return on Loblaw shares and commenting briefly on the 100% increase in Loblaws' dividends since 1961. By now though, the session had been going for more than three hours and Basford, who was in charge of seeing that all the committee members got their turn at questioning, was becoming visibly anxious to get through the roster. Urie didn't get another chance until a few minutes before the lunch break.

URIE: This question is supplementary to one I asked earlier. What wholesalers does your company own?

ROBERTSON: You refer, within the consolidated organization?

URIE: Yes.

ROBERTSON: It does not own any.

URIE: What wholesalers does it have an interest in?

ROBERTSON: It has an interest in Kelly Douglas.

URIE: What is the size of that interest?

ROBERTSON: I do not have the exact percentage. There are two classes of stock. There is a direct, controlling interest, I believe, in share control.

URIE: Are there any others? National Grocers?

ROBERTSON: It has an interest in National Grocers, and in York Trading.

URIE: Are these controlling interests?

ROBERTSON: Yes.

URIE: Do these organizations deal with independent retailers in competition with your groceterias?

ROBERTSON: I am not in the merchandising end.

GEORGE HUFFMAN (vice-president and general manager): I would say that is right.

URIE: Do these wholesalers purchase their supplies from the same suppliers as Loblaws purchases groceries from, by and large?

HUFFMAN: Yes.

URIE: Loblaw Groceterias does not purchase through any of the wholesalers which it owns, partially or otherwise?

HUFFMAN: They supply two or three of our stores because they are out of the distance where it would be economical to transport our own goods.

URIE: Do they sell to these stores at the same mark-up as they would to independent retailers?

HUFFMAN: I would think so. I could not be factual, but I would think they would.

URIE: Could you get that information for us, sir? Therefore, in your organization, there is one extra step involved when a merchant purchases his goods from York Trading, National Grocers or Kelly Douglas. There is one extra element of cost involved to that retailer, over that which prevails throughout your organization, except in a few cases?

HUFFMAN: Yes, on the surface it would appear that way. In our retailer organization we perform the same service as a wholesaler. When he operates he has a buyer and a warehouse and we have the same thing.

URIE: What would be the margin of profit involved as between your warehouse and retail store?

HUFFMAN: I would have to inquire.

URIE: Would you get that for us? Arising out of an earlier question, I understand that all the shares that the Loblaw parent organization — Loblaw Groceterias or Loblaw Ltd., I am not sure — are owned by George Weston Ltd. Is that correct?

MEECH: This is right.

URIE: And George Weston Ltd. is in a vast number of businesses?

MEECH: Yes.

URIE: Therefore, your organization has direct or indirect connections with many suppliers of goods that are purchased by your retailer organization. Is that correct?

MEECH: That would be correct.

URIE: Could you supply for this committee information concerning the purchases from companies owned by your parent company, the George Weston organization? That is all, Mr. Chairman.

BASFORD: I have a couple of questions. I have been waiting to ask about the George Weston organization. It was predicted in the *Globe and Mail* yesterday that the centennial project for Loblaw Groceterias was a merger with Weston. Is that correct?

MEECH: It is the first I heard of it, Mr. Chairman. It has been mooted and it has been, I think, almost requested by the financial community, but we in Loblaws are not that close to the George Weston Company that we would know.

BASFORD: If this came about, it would create a huge colossus in the food business?

MEECH: No more than it is now. It is just a different rearrangement.

BASFORD: The merger would not affect your share of market?

MEECH: No.

BASFORD: In line with the questions by Mr. Urie, I wonder if you could file with the committee a statement or chart showing the companies in which Loblaw Groceterias Co., Ltd. has an interest, and the degree of that interest; and the companies which have an interest in Loblaw Groceterias Co., Ltd., and the degree of that interest?

MEECH: Yes, we can do that.

It was a breakthrough that had been coming for some time. Although only a week before his company's appearance before the Senate/House committee, Metcalf had been his usual evasive self, leaving stockholders and investment analysts alike puzzled over the exact operating position of the company, signs of increasing disclosure were becoming more evident. No one could yet tell how profitable Loblaws was in Ontario compared with its operations in New York State or in the U.S. midwest because the company preferred to take the "consolidated" route, lumping all the retailing operations together rather than providing segmented information by market area. Analysts felt that consolidated figures in an organization so obviously complex as Loblaws and George Weston Ltd. could hide a multitude of sins and mistakes. Yet Loblaws had also come a considerable distance in meeting the fundamental disclosure requirements that had been suggested two years earlier by the Toronto Society of Financial Analysts. These included provision of gross revenue figures and comparative figures for previous years; a statement on the source and application of funds (accountants' terminology for the way you describe a company's cash flow); interim financial statements; and background information on long-term leasing arrangements.

By a combination of factual knowledge and some educated guessing, the outside world was starting to piece together the international Weston organization. At least in the investment community, those who actively followed the group, known appropriately as Westonologists, already knew the broad lines of control and corporate relationships, starting with Garfield Weston's principal holding companies, Wittington Investments in Canada and George Weston Holdings in the United Kingdom, and running down to principal operating subsidiaries such as National Tea in the United States and George Weston Foods in Australia. In the spring of 1966, the *Economist* newspaper printed an article which, with its typical drollery, it titled, "Garfield Weston: The Unknown Household Name." After brushing over the vast expansion moves Weston had overseen in the 1950s and 1960s, the newspaper speculated that he had a grand consolidation plan in mind. The idea, it said, was that Weston would elect to group his worldwide retailing interests under one banner (in effect, lumping Fine Fare, Loblaws, National Tea and, conceivably, Fortnum & Mason under one holding company banner) and his food processing, pulp and paper and packaging interests (including North American and European bakeries, Eddy Paper Co. and South Africa's Premier Milling) under another.

There was a certain logic in this, but it was not to be. The person who was much closer to the truth of the organization, as it turned out, was a stock analyst named Neil Baker of the small Montreal firm of Morgan, Ostiguy & Hudon. Baker had kept his nose to the grindstone while most other analysts and institutional investors had tired of trying to figure out the Weston empire, and in early 1966, he produced a massive report on George Weston Ltd. It involved a tremendous amount of sleuthing on his part and the kind of analytical dexterity that these days could only be had from a good computer program. Baker adjusted his figures for everything from occasional capital gains on the sales of assets to deferred taxes. And to his surprise, he found as he went along that Weston officials were more forthcoming than usual. Once investors saw the major findings of the report it wasn't difficult to figure out why. One of Baker's principal conclusions was that earnings for both George Weston Ltd. and Loblaw Companies Ltd. had been overstated. Another was that some subsidiary operations appeared to be under financial strain due to the parent organization's philosophical commitment to expansion. But having said this, Baker also claimed to detect signs of a turnaround in real earnings potential in the group and speculated that corporate performance might soon get up to industry averages. If that were the case, George Weston Ltd. and Loblaw stock could well be undervalued. George Weston A shares and Loblaw A shares, selling at $22-5/8 and $11-1/8 respectively around the time the report was published, should clearly be trading at a much higher price in relation to company earnings.

For Weston and Metcalf the message was clear. If secrecy was at one time a vital trait that could protect the group from competitors, it had now obviously become a wasteful exercise. By being too covert, the companies had been antagonizing, or at least ignoring, equity investors; these included institutions as well as small retail share buyers. Those institutions, it could also be noted, were the same ones that were occasionally being tapped by subsidiaries such as the group's real estate arm, Loblaw Leased Properties, for large wads of financing. Likewise, Baker's assumption that the group was under-performing was a sound one, even if his suggestion that a turnaround for the group was imminent turned out to be rather premature. Secrecy certainly wasn't doing anything to improve the bottom line.

Metcalf, giving a new meaning to one of his favourite office-wall slogans, "Attitudes are more important than facts," didn't exactly embrace the new philosophy of openness. At the George Weston Ltd. annual meeting in early June, 1966, and the Loblaw meeting in November, he sidestepped pointed questions with his usual ebullient dexterity. He was content to hint about the future, of expansion in U.S. retailing — the company had just purchased a Los Angeles food chain, Better Foods Inc. — and to talk of higher dividend payouts in the coming centennial year. But once the Senate/House Committee had made its request, the outcome was inevitable. Metcalf, in consultation with Weston, decided to get it over with at once by providing details on corporate organization and control not only to the committee, but to the nation's leading business newspaper, the *Financial Post*. Its December 10 issue trumpeted the scoop over two full pages: "Weston group unveils huge empire," and combined commentary with a detailed organization chart and a chronology of the group's development in North America. The outside world had all the major pieces of the puzzle; all it had to do now was to try to make sense out of them.

Just before Christmas, the Senate/House Committee tabled an interim report on food price trends. To a certain extent, it agreed with the original brief submitted by Loblaws that the reasons for food price inflation were many and varied and that it was impossible to pin the blame on any particular group, be they farmers, truck drivers or even supermarket owners. The committee did, however, argue strongly for clearer packaging, weighting and grading of products, and it took exception to the supermarket executives' overenthusiasm for promotional schemes. It also pushed for increased corporate disclosure, both by public and private companies. With particular reference to the Weston group's vast extent and presumed economic power, it suggested further investigation. This message was taken up in early January by consumer groups, who pressed the committee members to call in Garfield Weston. The committee considered the idea and then wisely declined. The cat, after all, was already out of the bag.

CHAPTER 8

The Interregnum

GARFIELD WESTON: *I feel real optimism, real*
optimism. We're going to have our greatest year
in 1972, yes?
TED CREBER: *Yes.*
GEORGE METCALF: *Yes.*
GARFIELD WESTON: *I like a man who knows how to*
say yes.

An exchange overheard by the
shareholders at the 1971 annual
meeting of George Weston Ltd.

Ln June of 1967, it looked as if
Garfield Weston was ready to make Canada his home base. With
the exception of a spell after the Second World War when he lived
in Vancouver, Weston had spent more than 30 years in the
United Kingdom, although he'd often demonstrated that if there
were a company to be bought or a segment of the empire that
needed attention he was only too willing to travel. Now it seemed
to be Canada's and North America's turn once again. Working
through Eastern Chartered Trust Co. he arranged to buy a
five-acre estate at 49 Country Lane in Toronto from stockbroker

George A. Richardson for slightly more than $283,000. The 14-year-old shale-stone split-level house was set in the city's York Mills district and featured a 26 foot by 17 foot living room, an 18 foot by 15 foot kitchen and a similar-sized den. It was far from being the most opulent property Weston had ever owned; at the time, for instance, he also held court occasionally at Barrettstown, a castle in County Kildare on the outskirts of Dublin. It was also true that Weston was as enthusiastic a dealer in residential properties as he was of companies; during his adult life, he probably owned more houses than most well-to-do people own cars. Yet by virtue of the Country Lane property's relative simplicity and modernity, its purchase could almost be considered a signal that Weston was getting back to basics. And in this mood his eyes had turned back to the New World.

Superficially, it was hard to figure out why Weston chose this time to return. Although the extent of his North American operations had been the target of criticism at the joint committee inquiry the previous December, the unaccustomed scrutiny had done them little if any harm. If anything, they looked uncommonly prosperous. Sales at George Weston Ltd. the previous year had risen an extremely healthy 19% to $580 million and earnings were up more than 12% to $15.3 million. At principal subsidiary Loblaw Companies, the story was much the same; sales for 1966 had jumped almost 12% to $2.4 billion and earnings were 13% higher at close to $22 million. The frenetic acquisition pace set by his chief Canadian lieutenant, George Metcalf, didn't seem to be hurting at all. Thanks to the cash generated by continuing operations, adroit sell-offs of those portions of acquired companies that didn't fit and successful issues of common and preferred stock and debentures over the years, the organization was far from being a financial cripple. George Weston Ltd. and Loblaw Companies, to the average business person, was a smoothly functioning organism whose only problem was that it was in danger of becoming too big and monopolizing the Canadian food trade.

Or was it? Despite his enormous regard for Metcalf's loyalty and service, Weston wasn't blind to the danger signals that had been reaching his office on the top floor of Fortnum & Mason in London. It was gradually becoming clear that Loblaw Groceterias, the group's principal Canadian food retailer, wasn't nearly as competitive as other firms like Dominion Stores Ltd. or Steinbergs Ltd. Loblaws' stores were smaller, their fixtures quaint and dull and, worst of all, their sales per square foot were declining. This same pattern was being repeated in the United States by key subsidiaries Loblaw Inc. in its western New York State and Pennsylvania stores, and at National Tea Co.'s stores in the U.S. midwest and south. Take-over activity at both George Weston Ltd. and Loblaws was considerably lighter than normal in 1967 (the major addition was a 96% holding in the fishery company, Connors Bros. Ltd. for an estimated $7.5 million. On the other side of the ledger, the company hived off a 31% chunk of its Fine Fare investment in the United Kingdom, selling it back to its original parent, Associated British Foods), so it might have been expected that more money would have been devoted to store modernization and rationalization. In fact, it wasn't.

There were other negative signs. The overall performance of Weston's Canadian food wholesaling companies looked fine but there were indications that they were starting to lose market share to more aggressive competitors. Likewise, the positive synergy one might have expected to develop from George Weston Ltd.'s ownership of food manufacturing and processing and Loblaw Companies' ownership of food retailing chains didn't seem evident. George Weston Ltd. had been only partly successful in selling its food products to food chains who were competing with Loblaws. Yet Loblaws wasn't buying enough of its food lines from Weston-owned companies. In other words, Garfield Weston's traditional quest for "tied accounts" — essentially sales among the various companies in his empire — was being frustrated.

When Keith Dalglish got the call in November, 1967, to fly to Britain to discuss George Weston Ltd.'s and Loblaw Companies' affairs with Garfield Weston, he was surprisingly unruffled at the prospect. The 37-year-old partner in the chartered accountancy firm of Thorne, Gunn, Helliwell & Christenson had been working on the audits of Weston's Canadian companies for the previous five years and he assumed that this overseas trip, in company with another Thorne, Gunn partner, R.J. Kane, was simply to give the boss a quick review of the North American end. It was perfectly logical that Dalglish would be chosen for such an exercise, in view of the fact that his role as auditor had made him privy to more of the group's secrets and peculiarities than any of its executives with the exception of Metcalf. Once settled in Weston's ornate London office, however, he realized that the meeting was going to be more than routine. In all, Dalglish spent three days in Weston's office going over the workings of Canadian and U.S. subsidiaries in intimate detail. Weston, restraining his normal high enthusiasm and assertiveness, listened intently throughout, and at the end of the third day he made Dalglish a surprising offer. Would he like to leave Thorne, Gunn to become vice-president and managing director of George Weston Ltd.? As such, his responsibilities would be primarily in the food processing and wholesale end — the retailing side would remain Metcalf's responsibility — but he would also be charged with setting up a program of financial planning and controls that would show top managers throughout the group how to keep track of costs and plan realistic profit targets. Laissez-faire was about to be replaced with the strictures of modern, professional management.

Dalglish was an intriguing choice. He was young and accomplished, having graduated from University of Toronto Schools in 1948 and then going on to an arts degree at the University of Toronto's Trinity College. Shortly after graduation in 1952 he joined the accountancy firm of Price Waterhouse, and by 1957 he was a full-fledged CA. In 1963 he moved to Thorne, Gunn where he was initiated into the Byzantine bookkeeping of the Weston group. His style, however, was very unWeston. In the past,

Garfield Weston had shown a predilection for aggressive, driving, almost charismatic managers to run his companies, the two best examples being George Metcalf and James Gulliver. Dalglish was tall, soft-spoken and genial. He hardly looked like the man who could reform one of Canada's biggest and most complicated conglomerates.

Still, the new general manager had reason to be confident that he could handle the job. Quite aside from his familiarity with the inner workings of the Weston group, he wasn't a total stranger to life outside the accountancy profession; from 1960 to 1962, he had served as the secretary-treasurer of a small Toronto computer company, ICT (Canada) Ltd. He also had a solid mandate from Garfield Weston. As he told a *Financial Post* reporter when he assumed his new title, "I want to plan where we'll be five years from now." It was a not so subtle message to cynics on Bay Street, who guessed that the appointment was an interim one that would give Metcalf time to straighten things out at Loblaws or allow Weston's youngest son, Galen (a newly minted Weston director now busily building his own chain of grocery stores in Ireland with direction from older brother Garry) time to mature in the family business.

Six months into the job, Dalglish's mandate was strengthened again when Garfield Weston named him president of George Weston Ltd. From the standpoint of the investment community, he was making all the right noises. He defended George Weston Ltd.'s and Loblaws' disclosure record and he downplayed the group's image as a monopolistic food ogre. Not only was the group comparatively paltry in size by American standards, Dalglish argued publicly, but there wasn't a single instance where it could effectively control markets or prices even if it wanted to. Although neither analysts nor investors were exactly thrilled with Weston group operating results in 1967 (George Weston Ltd. managed to post modest gains in sales and profits while Loblaw Companies slumped noticeably in both departments) they detected a new candour in the financial reporting. George

Weston Ltd.'s annual report that year was a refreshingly hype-free recitation of the various subsidiaries' operations and, to the surprise of some observers, it actually mentioned problems in such areas as forestry and fishing. The company also joined other progressive publicly traded firms by adopting deferred tax accounting (a bookkeeping method that accounts for taxes that aren't necessarily going to be paid in the current year, when compiling a company's income statement) which had the effect of understating rather than bloating profits.

As president, Dalglish could speak with even greater confidence of his plans to reshape the group. Having sized up the problems, he was putting further consolidation on hold and placing the emphasis on financial controls and planning so that each company could become a better defined profit centre. Growth from now on was to be steady and measured, and if there was an occasional slip from one year to the next, there wouldn't be any panic in George Weston Ltd.'s executive suite in the Canadian Imperial Bank of Commerce building on Toronto's King Street. Dalglish could afford to be this sanguine because he had developed a vision of the group's future. Henceforth, he predicted, the companies were going to stay away from the acquisition trail and the perils of retailing and concentrate more on growth from within, and on marketing efforts that would build brand loyalty to the hundreds of Weston-made products.

Dalglish quickly accumulated the talent to translate his plans into action. Leon Weinstein, 63, who'd been something of a floater in the group since his family's Power Supermarket chain had been bought by Garfield Weston in 1953, had agreed the previous year to act as president of Loblaw Groceterias, Loblaw Companies' Ontario retailing arm, for a period of two years to help shape things up. At Sayvette Ltd., Loblaw Companies' troubled bargain department-store chain, veteran merchandiser Abe Gold was brought in as president and chief executive officer. Gold, a former secretary-treasurer of Peoples Department Stores, staged a minor miracle by turning a Sayvette loss of $1.6 million in 1967 into a modest pre-tax profit of $216,000 the following year. Dalglish also made an important addition to George Weston Ltd.'s sparse head office staff by hiring a like-minded accountant, Philip Connell, as vice-president, finance. At 44, Connell had the right credentials to assist in the make-over. He'd won his spurs at Clarkson Gordon & Co. in the late 1940s and early 1950s and then gained corporate experience as comptroller at Canadian Westinghouse Co. Ltd. and later Domtar Ltd.

Given Dalglish's strong start, outsiders were stunned in the last week of January, 1969, when a brief press release informed them that Dalglish was being demoted to — the release actually used the words "has assumed the office of" — vice-president, finance, Connell's job. About a month later Dalglish left the Weston organization entirely, returning to a partnership at Thorne, Gunn. The new president and managing director was an even bigger surprise: veteran family and corporate counsel, George Edgar (Ted) Creber. It all happened so fast that some directors of Weston group companies admitted to being puzzled. But when many of them thought it over, Dalglish's abrupt plunge from grace began to make sense. He was never really an operations man in the first place and his vision of the company, his style, even his physical appearance, put him at odds with the man he had more or less replaced, George Metcalf. Metcalf was still in charge at Loblaw Companies and, from the moment Dalglish arrived, he had been in no mood to co-operate. "Some of the transitions were going to be severe and Metcalf and Dalglish disagreed," a former Loblaw executive recalls. "Metcalf wasn't good at handling the retail end, and there were a lot of unproductive people around. Keith wanted to do something about it, but George didn't. . . . Keith wasn't given the opportunity to do many of the things he wanted to do."

The question now was whether Creber would be given this opportunity. Once again, Garfield Weston seemed to have made an unusual choice. At 41, Ted Creber was intimately familiar with the affairs of the group companies and the family. He was a partner in the group's principal legal firm, Wahn, Mayer, Smith,

Creber, Lyons, Torrance & Stevenson, and had been a director of the Eddy Paper Co. since 1961 and of George Weston Ltd. since 1962. He also held vice-presidencies with the three concerns through which family control was exercised at the very top of the corporate pyramid — the W. Garfield Weston Charitable Foundation, Wittington Investments Ltd., and its real estate arm, Wittington Realty & Construction Ltd. Yet the very closeness of his relationship with the Westons, along with his limited experience running companies (he had served as a director of two small Ontario manufacturing concerns, Blue Mountain Pottery Ltd. and Viceroy Manufacturing Co. Ltd.) led many to suspect that his was an interim appointment, that his job was simply to hold things together until Galen was ready.

Looking back, Creber says that this was always the understanding, but he didn't dwell on it at the time. Instead, he gave every appearance of taking his job seriously and of preparing for the long haul. Physically, Creber was the antithesis of Dalglish. He was short and balding, but with a kind of lean athleticism that suggested deep reserves of energy. With his patrician features and unrevealing manner, it was initially tempting to dismiss him as a thin-lipped front man for Garfield Weston. This impression was only fortified by his unpretentious office and his clean-swept desk. But there were clues that more lay underneath. The stately equestrian prints that decorated his office hinted at his passion for the demanding and often dangerous sport of riding. And if his presentation was cool, it was because he'd transferred his tough and incisive legal style from the courtroom to the boardroom. He could be a very caring and dogged ally. Leon Weinstein remembers taking a flyer on some speculative stock in the early 1960s because he had been charmed by a young Vancouver promoter named Murray Pezim. Pezim not only told him he couldn't lose, he also gave Weinstein a written guarantee that he could get his money back. A few days later Weinstein told the story to Creber over lunch. Creber casually asked if Pezim was registered to sell stock in Ontario, and when Weinstein admitted he had no idea, the two went back to Creber's office to find out. In any event,

Creber pointed out, nobody was in a position to give guarantees on stock purchases. Phone calls were made, the last of which was to Pezim, and not long after Weinstein was told his investment was on its way back to him in a series of ten postdated cheques. Only after Weinstein pressed him did Creber agree to bill the Loblaw executive for his efforts. "He sent me a bill for $500," Weinstein says. "Most lawyers would have wanted to be partners in the deal."

Creber was aware that there was little to be gained in struggling with Metcalf, so he stuck mainly to the affairs of George Weston Ltd., even going so far as to chastise any group executives who sought to draw him unnecessarily into Loblaw business. In this he was wise, if only because so much needed to be done at the parent company. Essentially, Creber picked up Dalglish's torch, arguing from the beginning that what George Weston Ltd. and its subsidiaries needed was a move away from rapid expansion to steady, inwardly generated profit growth. This required, first of all, the drafting of planning and budgeting systems. Forecasting and reporting had to be refined in all areas of the group's operations and, in what could only be construed as an implicit criticism of Metcalf's management style, he pushed for greater inter-company co-operation, whether it was a question of intragroup sales or of banding together to make more efficient bulk purchasing arrangements. Such openness and teamwork clearly outweighed the value of secrecy or, as Creber put it at one stage, "Management was always concerned about information coming into the hands of a competitor, but I think a good competitor knows it anyway."

Working with Connell and a newly recruited team of executives at the George Weston Ltd. head office, Creber made substantial progress in a number of these areas in the first two years of his presidency. He also managed to win his subordinates' respect. "Ted Creber was a very capable person," says Connell, now an executive vice-president with a Loblaw competitor, Oshawa Group Ltd. "He was very incisive in his thinking; not very much got past him." This seemed to be the verdict of the stock market and the investment community. Creber took the trouble to court investors, improving George Weston Ltd.'s disclosure — he introduced annual results by division, for example, although he continued to resist consolidating Loblaw Companies' results in George Weston Ltd.'s figures — and making himself available to analysts and reporters alike. In this, he was often smart enough to be the first one to draw attention to corporate warts. When interviewers complimented him on George Weston Ltd.'s overall profit growth, Creber was likely to point out that the attractive total shouldn't disguise the fact that profit margins were actually declining.

If Garfield Weston was taking an active role in his Canadian companies in the early 1970s, he was operating strictly behind the scenes. The house at 49 Country Lane hadn't truly become his principal residence and when he visited corporate headquarters, Weston radiated a slightly eccentric elder statesman quality, dropping in from time to time to inspire his executives with upbeat rhetoric and gift bottles of his favourite pick-me-up, Vitamin E pills. He could still skirt the boundaries of good taste — at the George Weston Ltd. annual meeting in 1972, he took one last public shot at Britain's move to join the European Common Market. "It's the beginning of the end of that great organization known as the British Empire," he said. "Now we will have to compete with millions of Frenchmen working in the fields on their knees." Such unfortunate lapses aside, Weston seemed like a gentle chairman emeritus, content to bask in the praise of shareholders for whom he had provided a lifetime's worth of steady dividends.

That left Creber to take the brunt of the praise or the blame, and in the early part of the decade George Weston Ltd. attracted a reasonable amount of the latter. One instance was the corporation's unhappy investment in a large Ottawa-based food wholesaler, M. Loeb Ltd. which had operations extending across eastern Canada and into the United States and, consequently, was a major purchaser of Weston food products. It also owned a significant chunk of preferred stock in Canada's largest whole-sale drug distributor, National Drug and Chemical Co. of Canada Ltd. The story on Bay Street went that, in the fall of 1972, M. Loeb became irritated with Westons and, at one point, chairman Bertram Loeb decided he would no longer buy any of the group's products. Tempers supposedly grew so frayed that Garfield Weston himself flew over to settle the matter; his solution, naturally, was to buy out the Loeb family's holding. By the spring of 1973, George Weston Ltd. had quietly managed to pick up almost 19% of M. Loeb stock on the open market at a cost of slightly more than $5 million. M. Loeb's countermove in this undeclared and unacknowledged boardroom battle was to make an offer early that year to issue its treasury shares on a one-for-one basis for the stock of another company, Horne & Pitfield Foods Ltd., an Edmonton-based food wholesaler with operations in Alberta and the Northwest Territories. The message for any-one buying M. Loeb stock was clear: the owner-managers were going to dilute outside holdings and fight to retain control.

The corporate Goliath had stumbled across a David and the result was roughly similar to the outcome of the biblical story. Despite its now considerable shareholding, George Weston Ltd. had no appointees on the M. Loeb board, nor did it have the slightest say in M. Loeb's management. What's more, if it pressed on with stock purchases, Bertram Loeb might indeed deliver on his promise to stop buying bread and cakes. To make matters even worse, the federal Department of Consumer and Corpo-rate Affairs announced later in the year that it would investigate trading in M. Loeb shares because of its concern that fair competition in the food retailing business might somehow be threatened. Creber wisely decided to sell the M. Loeb holding, parcelling it out over several months in order to avoid depressing the share price — and thus George Weston Ltd.'s surrender value — too severely.

The M. Loeb affair wasn't George Weston Ltd.'s or Creber's only brush with the federal government in 1973. That August,

Eugene Whelan, then Minister of Agriculture, told a television interviewer that food prices, particularly for bread, were too high and that the consuming public was being victimized by manufacturers. "We say they don't need to go that high, but Westons or these big companies have got control of the bread manufacturing industry and they can just about damn well do what they please," he said. Whelan could be accused of making a little political hay, given the circumstances. Between 1971 and 1973, Canada had the world's second fastest growing economy after Japan. But real output gains in those years, which averaged slightly less than 7%, had a price. Swift growth was accompanied by a sharp increase in inflation, particularly in food prices, which moved from an annual rate of increase of 1.1% in 1971 to 14.6% in 1973. It was like the mid-1960s, but with a difference. Nationalist cabinet ministers such as Consumer and Corporate Affairs minister Herb Gray were specifically concerned that groups such as food producers and retailers were gouging the public, and they were also concerned that business was too concentrated, too powerful and inimical to the national interest. After the first oil-price crunch sent inflation skyward in late 1973, these concerns intensified and eventually produced such government actions as wage and price controls (beginning in 1975, and a Royal Commission on Corporate Concentration (1976), which would pay special attention to George Weston Ltd. It was altogether a bad time to be in business, but Whelan's charges didn't phase Creber. He came out swinging. "It doesn't bother me that the only firm he mentioned was Westons," he said when asked his reaction. "It was probably the only one he could remember .... Profits and sales in our bakery division are hardly large enough to warrant staying in the business, except that we're already in it."

Other issues kept recurring as well, the most obvious of which was George Weston Ltd.'s accounting methods. By the early 1970s, the Canadian Institute of Chartered Accountants (CICA) had included in its guidelines for public companies the requirement that controlled subsidiaries be consolidated. George Weston Ltd.'s then 60% stake in Loblaw Companies clearly qualified for full inclusion in the parent's income statement and balance sheet rather than being treated solely as a source of dividend income. To make matters worse for George Weston Ltd., the Ontario Securities Commission (OSC) and other provincial securities agencies made it policy that public companies follow the CICA guidelines. OSC vice-chairman Harry Bray made threatening noises at George Weston Ltd., saying that the commission might even refuse to okay future prospectuses needed to raise equity should the company not comply with the policy. Creber didn't give up without a fight. He gamely argued that the fair disclosure regulations of the Canada Corporations Act overrode the CICA's guidelines and that inclusion of Loblaws would "result in distortions which would not present the clearest picture to shareholders."

It was a losing battle. The combination of regulatory pressure, plus the fact that other major companies were coming around, made it inevitable that Loblaw Companies' income statement would have to be consolidated into its parent's. And when it happened in 1974, Creber's prediction that there would be distortion proved correct. George Weston Ltd.'s sales suddenly jumped more than three-and-one-half times to $4.7 billion and its net profits rose 21% to $42 million. The inclusion, if anything, tended to disguise the fact that Loblaw Companies was in deep trouble, a fact that was all too apparent to executives at the subsidiary, particularly the youthful chairman and managing director who had been struggling for a year and a half to set things right — Galen Weston.

CHAPTER 9

The Making of a Conglomerateur

"Is the chosen son the man who's really needed to lead Loblaws out of the wilderness? Who knows, but he's the only one who's going to get a chance to try. Basically, it's going to be one of the most interesting and difficult turnarounds in the history of the grocery business."

Anonymous retailing analyst, 1973

Loblaw Companies' fortunes visibly began to unravel during the price wars that gripped the Ontario food market in the second half of 1970. A discounting battle had been shaping up for almost two years, and now the supermarket chains were taking turns devising new pricing policies that would temporarily steal market share points from their rivals. On November 1, Dominion Stores Ltd. began a truly major offensive. It closed its Ontario stores for the day to allow managers and stockboys to sweep through the aisles and mark down listed prices by a stunning 12%. While Dominion's "Deep Discount" program made shoppers giddy with bargain purchases, it had a traumatic effect on the food retailing business. Other chains rushed to catch up, prompting Dominion to chop its price levels even further; at one stage the chain and its major competitors were adjusting prices on an hourly basis.

The real fury of the price war didn't last long, and by mid-December food prices were creeping back up. Yet the balance of power in the business had been fundamentally altered. If you looked at statistics for the Toronto area alone you could see that Dominion had gone from a 30% market share in October to an astonishing 49% in January. Smaller, aggressive chains such as Food City and Steinberg's Miracle Food Marts, which had been trying to grab discount-pricing leadership for the better part of a decade, had also made gains, although they were only in the 1% to 3% range. The big loser in all of this was Loblaw Groceterias Ltd., Loblaw Companies' principal operating subsidiary in the province. Between October, 1970, and January, 1971, its Toronto market share had been halved from 30% to 15%.

Although this was as low as Loblaws' share would go (it actually recovered to hold slightly more than 20% by late spring) the price war had exposed the chain's serious weaknesses. Of Loblaws' 454 Canadian supermarkets, just over half were in Ontario, the nation's biggest market. The problem was, however, that they tended to be smaller than their rivals' stores and were generally in less desirable locations. While chains like Miracle Mart had followed the development of new neighbourhoods in the suburbs, Loblaws was still mainly confined to urban core areas. Likewise, many of Loblaws' stores were badly in need of renovation both inside and out. Overall corporate shabbiness was reflected in the chain's inadequate staff training in specialized service areas such as vegetables and produce.

To add to Loblaws' woes, the chain lacked a coherent retailing strategy. Loblaws had been a price follower rather than a leader through the 1960s (a distinction that, oddly enough, it had shared with the now transformed Dominion Stores), and once the price war was declared it had no real marketing response. At the height of the battle, it attempted to counter Dominion's "We will not knowingly be undersold" slogan with the murky and dubious line, "Maxi-Save, Deep-Cut Prices." There didn't seem to be a single category in which Loblaws shone. Compared with Dominion and the rest, the chain suffered in every department from the freshness of its meat to customer service. And even though Loblaws slashed its prices in the latter stages of 1970 to the point where it was more than competitive, consumers never really perceived it as a serious discounter.

Loblaws limped along in this fashion through 1971 and into 1972, just as similar problems were surfacing at Loblaw Companies, 51.5% controlled U.S. subsidiary, National Tea Co. National Tea was a venerable chain that had grown from a small store in Chicago in 1899 to America's eleventh largest supermarket company in the early 1970s. The Loblaw interest dated from 1956, when George Metcalf had picked up a 27% holding from a director and company founder, and over the years had increased that to a controlling position by a complicated series of share swaps involving four different Weston-owned companies. Still, the National Tea that Loblaws first bought into was a far different company from the one it ended up running. In the late 1950s, under the leadership of a rotund veteran grocer, Harley V. McNamara, National Tea had gone on an expansion kick, opening new stores and expanding others in midwest and southern United States' urban markets including Minneapolis, St. Louis, New Orleans and Denver. McNamara had been so zealous, in fact, that he drew the attention of the U.S. Federal Trade Commission. The FTC brought an antitrust suit against the company, charging that its numerous acquisitions violated both the FTC Act and the Clayton Act. Eventually, in 1966, National Tea was slapped with an order that required the FTC's prior approval for any retail grocery acquisition for a ten-year period.

Fortunately for National Tea, the FTC order was retroactive to 1959 and so had only three years to run by the time it was officially proclaimed. Unfortunately, though, the National Tea expansion program that had been conducted by McNamara, who retired in 1961, and his successor, Norman A. Stepelton, emphasized the building of small stores on the order of 12,000 square feet at a time when aggressive competitors like Jewel Companies and Fisher Foods were putting up 16,000- to 22,000-square-foot outlets. Likewise, National Tea stretched itself too thin, preferring to try for a small piece of several markets rather than concentrating on a few. To make matters worse, the company resisted using discount pricing tactics through the late 1960s, with the result that its operating results steadily declined. Between 1966 and 1971, the company's sales remained virtually flat at roughly $1.2 billion a year while profits declined from $11.3 million to $7.6 million.

By July, 1970, Metcalf and Garfield Weston decided they couldn't tolerate the stagnation any longer. Stepelton was summarily ousted and F. Bruce Krysiak, who was then chief executive officer of Loblaw Inc., National Tea's 77%-owned chain in western New York State and Pennsylvania, was brought in as his replacement. Although Loblaw Inc. didn't appear all that healthy alongside such competitors as Tops Supermarkets in Buffalo, Krysiak had earned a reputation as a turnaround artist by more than doubling its profits to $2.9 million between 1968 and 1970. Now he was expected to work similar magic at National Tea's Chicago head office, even though the company's structure and competitive position suggested that he was about to take a bath in a sea of red ink.

In substance, this was the picture Galen Weston presented to his father after he'd evaluated Loblaw Companies in the summer of 1971. To make things worse, Loblaw Companies' debt, accumulated in the more than $200-million acquisition binge of the 1950s and 1960s, was rapidly becoming too big to handle. Between 1953 and 1967, for instance, Loblaw Companies had sold issues of long-term debentures on ten occasions, in the process raising $80 million. Beginning in 1973, those debentures were going to mature fairly regularly. Over the next four years, in fact, the company was going to have to pay off something like $50 million, consisting of older debenture issues as well as commitments taken on through associated companies in the Weston group. If operating results seriously crumbled, it looked as if the company wouldn't be able to meet its obligations to the Canadian and U.S. financial institutions that had staked it to these funds, let alone pay the dividends on the various issues of preferred stock that it had sold over the years to many of those same institutions. At the same time, Garfield Weston and his son had to figure out where they were going to find the vast amount needed for store renovations as well as for maintaining the all-important dividend payout to common stockholders.

No doubt too, they discussed other aspects of George Weston Ltd.'s North American operations. In Canada, Sayvette and G. Tamblyn Ltd., the drugstore chain, were continuing to lose money, and the other divisional pillars of George Weston Ltd. were beginning to look a trifle fragile as well. The fisheries division, consisting of Connors Bros. on the east coast and B.C. Packers Ltd. on the west, was producing sales gains, but through much of the 1960s profits had been relatively low and the business was notorious for its cyclical swings. The same could be said of Weston's forest products concerns, Eddy Paper Co. and Eastern Fine Paper Inc. Changes in industry selling prices and periodic labour troubles made for abrupt swings in profits from year to year. Weston's food processing companies were also not immune to troubles, if only because there was considerable duplication of brands and manufacturing facilities.

With George Metcalf running Loblaw Companies and Ted Creber sticking closely to food processing and resources over at George Weston Ltd., overall the corporation lacked direction and purpose. The fundamental split in the organization between retailing and production was getting wider instead of narrower. And as was now only too clear, so long as Metcalf remained at Loblaw Companies, that side of the business was going to be in the doldrums.

The word in the higher ranks at Loblaws was that Galen Weston was reluctant to take an operating job at Loblaws as long as Metcalf was still around. That hurdle was at least partially overcome in an extraordinary meeting that took place in November of 1971 in the modest Toronto offices of Wittington Investments, the family holding company through which Garfield Weston exercised control of George Weston Ltd. and Loblaw Companies. Along with Garfield and Galen Weston, those attending the session included George Metcalf, Ted Creber and Phil Connell. In a sense, this crisis session only confirmed a plan the elder Weston and Metcalf had been discussing for weeks, that Galen would replace Metcalf as chief executive officer of Loblaw Companies, leaving Metcalf the chairmanship and continuing responsibility for National Tea, Sayvette and G. Tamblyn. As well, Metcalf was delegated to plan George Weston Ltd.'s new head office building on Toronto's St. Clair Avenue.

The meeting also dealt with Loblaw Companies' looming financial crisis. From Galen Weston's standpoint, Loblaw's debt crunch had to be alleviated before he could make any serious changes in the company's operating structure and style. The massive debt obligations threatened to bleed off every available dollar, and covenants agreed to with some lenders restricted the company's ability to act. The most inhibiting of these was a deal that had been arranged through a Loblaw financing arm, Glenhuron Properties Ltd. In 1955, Glenhuron had raised $33 million from a group of American insurance companies, which it then used to buy a leasehold interest in many of Loblaw Groceterias' store properties. This didn't bother the U.S. insurers because they inserted a trust indenture in the financing that restricted Loblaw Groceterias' ability to sub-lease, sell or do anything else with those properties until the money was paid back.

Common sense told Galen Weston that any major shake-out at Loblaw Companies was bound to involve a lot of store closures. But as long as those Glenhuron notes were outstanding, and as of late 1971, $26.5 million of them still were, his hands were tied. Now, however, the complex corporate structure that had allowed Loblaw Companies to build a massive debt load in the first place was turned to advantage to help bail the company out. Using stock in National Tea, G. Tamblyn and Glenhuron as collateral, Loblaw Companies arranged a $27-million term bank loan, which it used to retire the notes. To cover off this new loan, and get a bit of breathing room as well, Loblaw Companies then struck a deal with a Wittington Investments subsidiary, Wittington Realty & Construction Ltd., under which Wittington Realty would buy a number of Loblaw mortgages and properties for $35 million. One of those properties, amusingly enough, was the Loblaw Companies' head office on the Toronto lakeshore.

There were many other deals and asset shuffles; between 1968 and 1974 George Weston Ltd. and various associated companies would manage to pump no less than $164 million into Loblaw Companies. The Glenhuron property deal was pivotal because it gave Galen Weston room to manoeuvre, and with the help of two new associates, David Nichol and Richard Currie, that's exactly what he proceeded to do. Galen Weston acted as a serene but involved overseer while Nichol and Currie jumped into the executive trenches (their respective titles at the time were director of corporate development and director of profit development) and among the three of them, they made some crucial decisions in early 1972 about the Ontario operations of Loblaws. The first move was to gradually bring in new management blood at all levels of the organization, mainly by hiring experienced professionals from the United States. The second was to start closing stores; within months roughly 100 small outlets had been identified as suitable candidates. Next, Loblaws hired Vickers & Benson to develop an advertising campaign that would shatter the chain's image as a chronic price follower. It was the first time that Loblaw Companies had seen the need to use somebody other than its own in-house advertising specialists. Another outside firm, communications consultants Break, Pain and Wall Ltd. were hired to devise a new corporate identity that would see the classic yellow exterior tiles of Loblaws' stores with their block lettering replaced by a bold new orange and red "L" logo. Soon the insides of the stores were getting a similar make-over at the hands of a talented young designer, Don Watt.

The whole program was summed up by Loblaws' new marketing slogan, "More than the price is right ... but by gosh the price is right," which reflected the broad objective Weston and his cohorts had in mind. The point of the exercise was not just to rationalize and consolidate a losing grocery store chain, but to remake the image of the chain in the eyes of the public. Weston wanted Loblaws to stand for the most competitive prices and for the highest quality and best selection of groceries as well as of non-food merchandise.

On one level it seemed to work. Loblaws' market share in Toronto slowly but steadily climbed higher until early 1974 when it captured 25% of the business, almost as much as Dominion Stores. Progress on the income statement was considerably slower, however. Ontario sales continued to slip overall, going from $324 million in 1972 to $315 million two years later. When added into the results for other Canadian retail operations such as Zehr's Markets and O.K. Economy Stores, the net result was a loss of $1.2 million in 1972 and of roughly $100,000 in 1974.

Weston and his two young executive sidekicks, who by now were billing themselves as "change agents," remained optimistic. The signs of a turnaround in Ontario, and indeed across Canada, were clearly there; with enough investment and enough merchandising skills, Loblaws' bottom line would one day no longer match the red of its logo.

The problems in Canada seemed easier to cope with than those in the United States. For a time, Krysiak appeared to have the same brilliant touch at National Tea that he'd shown at Loblaw Inc. Despite all the odds, National Tea's profits rose from $7.6 million in 1971 to almost $9 million a year later. The National Tea annual report that year described him as a "master strategist" whose "dynamic leadership" was responsible for the company's revival. And at a massive party held at Toronto's Royal York Hotel in February, 1973, to celebrate Garfield Weston's seventy-fifth birthday, Krysiak sat at the head table on the right hand of Garfield himself, basking in the old man's compliments.

Barely a month later he was gone, fired by Galen Weston for failing to keep up National Tea's momentum. After March 31, 1972, when National Tea's last fiscal year had ended, trading results for the company steadily worsened. Indeed, in the fiscal year that was just ending, the company was headed for a slight decline in sales to $1.2 billion and a net loss of $9 million. Despite closing 146 obsolete stores in less than a year and making strenuous efforts to streamline operations, Krysiak was obviously not living up to expectations. Heading for what he described as a "sabbatical," the bitter executive charged that his favoured treatment at Garfield Weston's birthday party was the equivalent of a Mafia don's "kiss of death."

If anyone administered the kiss of death to Loblaws' U.S. operations, it was another grocery baron, Great Atlantic & Pacific Tea Co. chairman and CEO William J. Kane. In early 1972, under Kane's leadership, A & P had triggered an intense price war in some 35 U.S. states. A & P's bold price-cutting program, dubbed "Where Economy Originates" or WEO as it came to be known, was an attempt by the giant of the U.S. industry to shake itself out of the slow growth that had afflicted it through the 1960s. For eight years, A & P had been steadily losing ground to more aggressive chains such as Safeway Stores and Kroger Stores Ltd., and now it sought to recapture customers with one major discounting initiative. As it turned out, A & P's timing couldn't have been worse. Thanks mainly to rising inflation, the grocery industry had already suffered a few years of depressed profits; now, under the U.S. Economic Stabilization program that had been announced by President Richard Nixon in the fall of 1971, they were constrained from passing on to consumers increases in their operating costs. The result of all these factors was that in 1972 total U.S. food industry profits shrank to $3.9 billion from $7.9 billion the previous year. At A & P, a company whose structure and operating problems were those of a National Tea writ large, the outcome was even more disastrous. Despite sales of more than $6 billion in fiscal 1973, it lost more than $50 million.

National Tea was just one of many chains unfortunate enough to be pulled into A & P's discounting whirlpool, a point that was of cold comfort to both Galen Weston and Richard Currie as they shuttled back and forth between Toronto and Chicago. Their first priority was to replace the four corporate vice-presidents who'd walked with Krysiak, a task that led them to revamp the U.S. company's management team. By the fall of 1973, National had a new head, James A. Watson, the recently fired president of a competing chain, Gamble-Skogmo Inc. of Minneapolis, and a brace of new senior executives, some of whom came from a Gamble-Skogmo subsidiary, Red Owl Stores, Inc. (In 1974, Gamble-Skogmo and Red Owl went to court in an unsuccessful attempt to get a damage settlement from National Tea for pirating talent.) Once the new team settled in, it embarked on a store closure and modernization program similar to that of Loblaws in Ontario. In the next two years, some 200 stores were abandoned and scores of others were renovated. And in 1975 and 1976, with price wars flaring up and inflation still hurting on the cost front, National decided to get out of Denver, Davenport, Iowa, and its home market, Chicago. Finally rendered as lean as one of its barbecuing steaks, National Tea managed in 1977 to get back in the black.

By this time, the managerial fireworks were largely over. Management positions and many directorships had changed throughout the Weston companies. At head office, the aging Metcalf had been relegated to a ceremonial vice-presidency, a job in which he continued to work long days, although with declining impact. In addition to holding the chairmanship of Loblaw Companies, Galen Weston also became, in 1974, chairman and managing director of George Weston Ltd. As he put it, he was "stepping back from the hurly-burly," satisfied that the weak links in the organization were being strengthened. He was right about the corporation's improving health, but in the end it took longer than he would have liked. Loblaw Companies suffered mightily from 1973 through 1976, when it posted a net loss of $21.7 million, its worst performance ever. Naturally, the problems percolated through to George Weston Ltd.'s income statement, and in 1976 it posted a loss of $15 million, the first and so far only loss in its history. Galen Weston had been the presiding surgeon at one of the greatest corporate lipectomies in Canadian history. The operation was successful but the patient had taken a long time to recover and the cost was high.

On October 22, 1978, Garfield Weston died in Toronto's Wellesley Hospital after suffering a massive heart attack. He'd been in Toronto to visit his children, and until the moment he was struck down had seemed to be in good health. Only eight months before, he had been robust enough to host at his Pompano Beach, Florida, apartment, a weekend series of parties to celebrate his eightieth birthday. Now the obituary writers were trundling out all the old anecdotes, recalling everything from his flamboyant purchase of Spitfire fighter planes for the British government during the war to his pro-apartheid convictions. Squeezed in between were tributes to his strong family values and to the sense of divine guidance that had sprung from his Wesleyan roots. As he was laid to rest in the southeast corner of Toronto's vast Mount Pleasant cemetery, the area of spacious plots reserved for the city's aristocracy, he was already being reduced to a figure more memorable for his eccentricities than for his real accomplishments.

In 1972, five years after the death of Reta Weston, he had married again, this time to a Spaniard 35 years his junior, Marguerite Martin de Montoya. Thereafter, he devoted more time to raising race horses at his estate in Ireland, periodically producing contenders for the Epsom Derby and other major races, as well as indulging in occasional and unpredictable acts of charity. In 1976, for instance, he bought a major Group of Seven painting, Tom Thomson's "Woodland Waterfall," at auction for $285,000 and promptly donated it to the McMichael Canadian Collection in Kleinberg, Ontario. The gesture was typically Weston, done with a generous impulsiveness that recalled such other gifts as his donation of $1 million for medical research to the Banting and Best Institute at the University of Toronto in the 1960s.

In his last years he had largely retreated from the public, intent as always on preserving his sense of privacy. When he was in the news, it was usually for some act that merely reinforced his image as a tycoon, and an increasingly irascible one at that. Just before Christmas, 1977, as he cruised the aisles of the women's fashion department at Fortnum & Mason, two women customers approached him with a 150-name petition requesting that the store not alter the look of its venerable watering hole, the Spanish Bar. The bar had been recently closed following the retirement of its two head barmen, and customers had begun speculating that a remodelling was on the way. Weston, who initially thought the two were presenting him with some sort of tribute, wasn't about to enlighten them about any such plans. Once he realized they were giving him a petition, in effect seeking to influence the way he ran his personal corporate sanctuary, he threw it under a table and angrily dismissed them. As one of his petitioners later remarked, "It never crossed my mind that this benign old gentleman could be so vitriolic."

In his final years Garfield Weston looked to the future rather than dwelling on the past. And nowhere was this fact more evident than in his succession planning at Associated British Foods and George Weston Ltd. Before his death, he could rest easy in the knowledge that the family had enough shares in both conglomerates to assure ongoing control. It was even more satisfying to know that Garry was securely and competently in charge at ABF and that Galen, his trial by fire at Loblaws now behind him, was leading George Weston Ltd. into a prosperous third generation of growth. Garfield Weston would have revelled in the Canadian company's results the year he died. Its 14% sales jump to $5.2 billion and its 78% rise in profits to $57 million would have given him the stuff of a vintage annual meeting speech.

After Loblaws had been turned around, it seemed that Galen

Weston could do no corporate wrong. On the one occasion when he did veer toward a major blunder, the divine power was as kind to him as it had been to his father. In the late 1970s, the major players of corporate Canada went into a kind of frenzy. Inflation was eroding earnings, pushing up operating costs and depressing the market value of physical assets. Any CEO who took the trouble to analyze the trend quickly came to the conclusion that the best way to grow wasn't to invest in new productive assets, but to buy existing ones that were going cheap. Such was the rationale for the enormous merger and take-over binge that dominated Canadian business into the early 1980s.

Students of business power who were still reeling from the findings of Robert Bryce's Royal Commission on Corporate Concentration in 1976 viewed the take-over mania with growing alarm and they were partly justified. Between 1978 and 1981, acquisitions eliminated more than 50 major public firms from the Toronto Stock Exchange's 300 Index. It had reached the stage where a mere 25 industrial companies controlled roughly one-third of Canada's productive assets. Moreover, the nation's financial institutions were only too happy to aid and abet the asset grab. Although they would come to rue their freewheeling lending once a major recession devastated the economy in late 1981, bankers in the heat of the action seemed to feel that the only thing better than a $50 million loan was a $100 million one.

Under the circumstances, it was easy to dream of turning a massive enterprise into a mega-enterprise, to use the prefix that was most popular in the period. This is exactly what Galen Weston was doing in the late summer of 1978. Through Wittington Investments, he quietly began buying stock in the Hudson's Bay Co., a widely held retailer with admirable prospects whose 309-year history had had much to do with the development of the Canadian nation. The Bay may have had its roots in the fur trade, but now it was a solid department-store chain that was growing stronger by the month. That October it won control of a smaller retail chain, Zellers Ltd., and before the year was out it was going after another senior retailing company, Simpsons Ltd.

Thanks to his experience operating Brown, Thomas in Ireland, Weston was no stranger to department stores. Now, as he worked through the basic numbers, he could see grand possibilities in a merger. If The Bay and George Weston Ltd. were one, Wittington would control annual Canadian sales of $7 billion, an amount equivalent to more than one-quarter of the country's food and department stores' sales and roughly equal to 10% of all retail sales, including automobiles. Such an entity, assuming the positive earnings projections for both were correct, would throw off vast amounts of cash flow and provide enormous leverage in every aspect of retailing and food processing, whether it was in arranging volume discounts from suppliers or in being able to fend off competitors. Weston even looked favourably on The Bay's oil and gas interests and considered that they'd be not a bad fit with George Weston Ltd.'s existing resource interests in forest products and fishing. The worst that could happen was that he could sell off The Bay's resources arm, Hudson's Bay Oil and Gas Co. Ltd., and its real estate development subsidiary, Markborough Properties Ltd., and concentrate on expanding the department-store network. Considering the health that had been restored to George Weston Ltd.'s balance sheet and the fact that the company was generating a cash flow of roughly $150 million a year, The Bay purchase also looked eminently financeable.

That's also how it looked to Kenneth Thomson, heir to the title Lord Thomson of Fleet and master of the international media and energy conglomerate that he had inherited from his father, Roy Thomson. The Bay wasn't quite the complementary fit for Thomson that it was for Weston, but its prospects were sufficiently appealing that on March 1, 1979, two of Thomson's investment companies, Woodbridge Co. and Thomson Equitable (International) Ltd., announced a $31 a share bid for 51% of the company's shares for a total value of about $365 million. The Bay's directors were slightly surprised (although not greatly so, given that any widely held company at the time could be considered vulnerable to a take-over attempt) and then angered. As they pointed out in a circular to shareholders later that month, the company's profit outlook over the next five years would suggest that $37 to $40 would be a more appropriate value for the shares.

Weston too was surprised by the Thomson bid, but by the end of March he'd rallied enough to prepare a bid of his own, a much more agreeable $40 a share for 51% of the company, payable in cash; Weston preferred stock or a combination of stock and cash. The total value of the bid: $488 million. The offer was conditional on Weston's getting all the shares he sought. Two days later Thomson amended his offer, jumping to $35 a share and enlarging the net by saying that he would buy up to 60% of the company's stock. Now the decks were cleared for a polite but vicious boardroom battle. First Weston alleged that Thomson's revised bid was really a new bid and that it wasn't leaving stockholders enough time to properly make up their minds. After the Ontario Securities Commission met with both sides, Weston withdrew his complaint and Thomson extended the time limit on his revised offer. Next, in early April, Weston approached institutional investors about an escrow arrangement under which stockholders could deposit shares for either offer. The OSC rejected that plan because it considered it would constitute a material change in Weston's offer. To complicate things still further, the Thomson interests then charged that Weston's offer of the escrow arrangement was contravening not only the Ontario Securities Act, but the Canada Business Corporations Act. The Thomson companies, meanwhile, had amended their offer to $37 a share for up to 75% of The Bay's outstanding shares.

Thomson was determined, and in the end Weston wasn't. On April 9, Galen Weston said he wouldn't amend his offer any more and suggested that Bay stockholders tender their shares to Thomson. In hindsight, it was a wise move for several reasons. At the time, it averted the possibility of even more intense scrutiny than the OSC had already levelled at the deal. As the bidding war had heated up, the federal department of Consumer and Corporate Affairs had grown increasingly interested; if Weston emerged triumphant, there might have been an investigation to see if such a corporate combination would restrict competition. From a longer perspective, Weston was smart not to saddle the corporation with the kind of debt needed to purchase The Bay. The skyrocketing interest rates that gripped the country in the early 1980s would have strained the balance sheet. Shortly after the Thomson deal, The Bay rapidly turned from a silk purse into a sow's ear. Its retailing strategy unsure, its oil and gas holdings devastated in the wake of the National Energy Program and the 1981-82 recession, and its balance sheet almost sunk by the debt it had taken on to finance its earlier acquisitions, the company was crippled for years.

Not so George Weston Ltd. and Loblaw Companies, however. Somehow, the battle for The Bay was a cathartic experience for Galen Weston and his top managers, perhaps because it reminded them of a crucial decision they had taken back in the darkest days of the Loblaw turnaround. It was simply that food processing, and retailing especially, were the direction they should take. Once the take-over play was over, the Weston group reverted to form and in so doing became the darling of Bay Street as well as Canada's most successful and innovative grocers. To borrow from their own sloganeering, the basic business of the company was right after all.

CHAPTER 10

Rolling in the Aisles

It was one of those three glorious Saturdays of the year when Dave Nichol's Insider's Report *is published in newspapers across Canada, and Nichol, as he is wont to do, was strolling through the Loblaws at Bayview and Moore avenues in Toronto. As the one and only media superstar ever to emerge from the grocery business, he wasn't in the least fazed when a middle-aged woman presented herself and began to describe her passion for Greek salads and then to bemoan the fact that Loblaws was no longer carrying President's Choice black olives, the best she'd ever used in her recipe. Nichol looked her in the eye and said simply, "Were they pitted or unpitted?"*

"Unpitted," she replied.

Nichol took out a small notebook and jotted down the particulars. A month later the unpitted olives were back on shelves.

Dave Nichol didn't become the heart-throb of the shopping cart set because he has the good sense to respond to a reasonable request from a customer. After all, giving the customer what she or he wants has been the basis of good business since time immemorial. His success isn't just due to the fact that he can move olives from grove to shelf in only a month in an organization as large and complex as Loblaw Companies. When the right people are in charge, conglomerates needn't be sluggish. It isn't even due to his ability to go a good idea one better. The June, 1987, edition of the *Insider's Report*, a gag-riddled, comic-laden handout that goes to about 10 million North American homes three times a year, featured a tribute to President's Choice Super Colossal Pitted Black Olives at $1.99 for a 14-ounce jar under the warning "Be careful how you lift them — You don't just pop these into your mouth, you hoist them."

Nichol can only pray that someone will disregard the instructions and get a hernia, if only because such news would make great reading in the next *Insider's Report*. It would also give Nichol just the excuse he needs to sell the handmade olive hoists that he will by then no doubt have accidentally discovered while cruising among the more remote Greek islands. If this sounds a trifle far-fetched, remember that this is the marketing wizard who in the last two years has convinced countless yuppies that they simply must have balsamic vinegar for their salads, Swiss water process decaffeinated coffee so they can sleep at night and Senior dog food if their pooches happen to be seven years of age or more.

Nichol is an executive vice-president of Loblaw Companies and his job is to run a subsidiary called Loblaw International Merchants Ltd. Its mandate — his mandate — is to comb the world for unique and tantalizing products as well as developing imitations of national brand items such as Coca-Cola and Oreo cookies and Tide detergent that are supposedly better than the originals. Production of these items can be undertaken almost anywhere in the world, through Weston-owned companies or not, depending on who provides the best quality and the greatest efficiency. Mixed in with this eclectic mixture of food items is a carefully selected range of hard goods — everything from Bulgarian wine goblets and nickel-plated Italian nutcrackers to

German dinner ware and virgin rubber garden hoses. In bringing all these things to our attention, Nichol has become, as one headline writer aptly put it, the "human face" of Loblaws. He is the visible grocer who, like those earnest, aproned young men of an earlier generation such as T.P. Loblaw and Milton Cork, let us know that we're dealing with people rather than with some vast impersonal corporation. But Nichol is more than a symbolic proprietor who's been miraculously teleported to the supermarket aisles; he's also a skilful and entertaining marketer who knows precisely how to share the fantasy, a success symbol who's able to pitch us his version of the good life every time he and his disturbingly unphotogenic French bull dog, Georgie Girl, encourage us to try President's Choice Belgian Waffles or Passionata blended fruit drink from France.

One look at the number of President's Choice items inside a typical urban middle-class kitchen tells you that Nichol is doing something right. Another sign is the fact that normally sophisticated, highly educated people will talk about the contents of an *Insider's Report* with a zeal that as teenagers they used to reserve for the naughty bits in D.H. Lawrence. Then there are Loblaw Companies' buoyant sales. Altogether, Loblaw Companies' Canadian retail subsidiaries sell close to $2.9 billion of groceries a year, roughly 9% of the nation's total food bill. Nichol's success is the visible emblem of a broad and well-developed retailing strategy that Loblaw Companies is using to secure its place in a shifting and often unpredictable food retailing industry.

That the industry has changed radically in the last decade is indisputable. Consider the fate of Dominion Stores, a market leader in the mid-1970s that has been chopped up and sold to Loblaws and The Great Atlantic & Pacific Tea Co. Dominion, one could argue, was the victim of the merciless competition and low margins that have always characterized the grocery business. But the underlying dynamics of the market have altered greatly too, reflecting shifting consumer concerns and expectations. The days are long gone when families got in their cars on Saturday morning and headed for their local supermarket to buy their food for the coming week. In the same way that department stores discovered that customers were willing to favour small boutiques with their business, the major food chains saw good chunks of their trade move to smaller convenience stores and specialty food outlets. Even though a predominant share of the business was still left to the supermarkets, this was being eroded by superstores, mammoth 50,000 square feet and larger outlets that were adapted from a European precursor, the hyper-marché.

This change in shopping patterns has been paralleled by a change in consumer habits and preferences. Once upon a time, grocers believed that the quickest route to increased turnover was a reduction in prices. All you needed to do to prove it was to close up for a few hours, mark everything down and declare a price war against your competitor down the street. If that didn't work, you got business by having the best, which is to say most convenient, location. Price and location remain important factors in determining a store chain's success, but as a major survey by the Grocery Products Manufacturers of Canada (GPMC) in the spring of 1987 demonstrated, other factors carry more weight with consumers. The GPMC asked 1,000 shoppers to name the things that made them buy, and topping the list of responses was product freshness. The second most important item was having a clean, well-lit store. Price came third. Ranking after these points, in descending order, were friendly service; a wide range of products; convenient hours; fast check-out; and finally, convenient location. The survey also found that while people prefer being able to make bulk purchases and to have their choice of house brand products, these aren't at the top of the list.

The GPMC responses are in line with the tastes of an influential group of consumers that's come to be known as the "wellness generation." Obsessed with health and fitness, they have shopping patterns that reflect these concerns, though they still demand low prices and good service. They display an apparently conflicting desire to have a nutritious diet relieved by the occasional indulgence. The low-fat yogurt and salad eaters want to be able to cap an evening out with a visit to a restaurant that specializes in flagrantly calorific desserts. They also want to be able to shove a handful of, say, President's Choice Extra Chocolate Chip Cookies down their throats at bedtime without suffering pangs of guilt.

The other point that needs to be made about the changing nature of the market is that the traditional distinctions between food retailers and other retailers have blurred considerably. Goods that used to be the preserve of department-store chains such as The Bay or Eaton's or of more specialized chains such as Canadian Tire are showing up in supermarkets. Thus the food chains are carrying a wider range of merchandise on which they can charge much higher markups than consumers would accept on food.

The supermarket chains are flexing newly developed muscles. They used to be like the proverbial 98-pound weakling on the beach, taking whatever the big national brand product companies dished out and having to like it. Until recently producers like General Foods, Nabisco Brands and Procter & Gamble, backed by their large-scale advertising and marketing programs, could easily get stores to carry and promote their wares because of perceived consumer demand. But over the last decade, the effectiveness of national brand advertising has diminished, thanks to everything from television remote controls that allow viewers to "zap" commercials to changes in eating habits that have seen consumers increasingly prefer fresh foods to the frozen, canned and otherwise processed varieties. Likewise, the high inflation of the 1970s taught retailers a bitter lesson about their relationship with national brand producers, in that for a long time it was the chains rather than the manufacturers that were left holding vast and costly inventories of unsold products. When the retailers came to their senses, they realized that they were carrying the ball for products whose saleability was exaggerated in the first place.

Ever so gradually, retailers began to sense that the power to determine what was going to be put on the shelves and how hard it was going to be sold was falling into their hands. In the early 1980s, as major retailers became fewer in number and were armed with better merchandising techniques and computers for analyzing their business flow, their power only increased. When they looked at what was happening in other countries they could see an alternative to buying from brand companies: they could make their own. Executives at Loblaw Companies, particularly Galen Weston, were drawn to the example of Marks & Spencer, a U.K. clothing and food store chain that has managed to elevate dowdiness to a fine art, yet can get people to spend billions of pounds a year on its house brand products produced under the St. Michael label. Likewise, Loblaws eyed the gains being made by one of Associated British Foods' major U.K. competitors, J. Sainsbury, and noted that a food retailer could do well by combining an active house brand program with large-scale, modern supermarket management.

Which is where Dave Nichol and the Loblaw Companies' strategy comes into play. At the high end, the sybaritic, indulgent end of the food market, Nichol and his staff, notably Jim White, the former food columnist for the *Toronto Star* and the man who really writes the copy for the *Insider's Report*, supply the entertainment and sex appeal that get people into the stores in the first place. Underlying their efforts is the extensive house brand program that Loblaw Companies has been building for years. At this writing, the President's Choice label has been affixed to as many as 472 products, including a subspecies called Teddy's Choice of 31 products for children ranging from cereal to baby oil. For each and every product, Loblaws can build in low production and marketing costs by sourcing them as efficiently as possible and by using the *Insider's Report* rather than expensive advertising campaigns to promote them. These advantages allow Loblaws to undercut significantly the price of national brand products.

The $1.4 billion capital spending program that Loblaw Companies began in 1985 means that all these bargains will increasingly be sold in newer, bigger and brighter stores than ever before. In 1986, for instance, Loblaw Companies spent $371 million on its system, covering everything from acquisitions of smaller chains (in this case $82 million to buy 26 Kroger Stores in the U.S. and six Capital Stores in Nova Scotia), new warehousing facilities and data processing and administration services. The lion's share, 60% of the total, went to new store development, especially eight new "combination" stores, massive 100,000 square foot plus outlets that have both food and general merchandise including clothing, cosmetics, pharmaceuticals and photo supplies.

An analysis of Loblaw Companies' retail operations shows that, while the total square footage of retail space isn't changing very much from year to year — if anything, it's contracting ever so slightly — the average store size is increasing. In 1984, the company's average store size was slightly more than 24,000 square feet; in 1986 it was almost 28,500 square feet. In 1984, the company had only eight stores that were larger than 60,000 square feet; in 1986 that number had risen to 18. When you combine such outlets with warehouses that can locate, sort and move thousands of items by the hour, and with a brilliantly run in-house label campaign, the capital investment looks eminently worthwhile. In 1985 and 1986, average sales per square foot in Loblaws' various chains jumped more than 14% to $457 while overall retail sales increased by over 21%. As followers of the company take pains to point out, the returns from all this building and development haven't yet reached their maximum level.

So far Loblaw Companies has the competition beat, but the other chains, from A & P through to Steinbergs and Super Carnaval, are fighting back strongly. While Loblaw Companies has contributed handsomely to the consolidated sales column of George Weston Ltd., it's arguable that the retailer's approach has been less than perfect. One estimate has it that only about 10% of the products Dave Nichol uses to tantalize consumers come from Weston-owned factories, for instance. Another point is that the proportion of intercompany sales in the George Weston group, at just 3% of the total, hasn't grown in a decade.

From Nichol's perspective these are tiny clouds over an otherwise pleasing landscape; he's been through much worse. At 47, he along with Galen Weston and Richard Currie can remember how hard it was to bring the Loblaw Companies back from the brink. He was the hard-nosed marketer and store renovator of the early days, the one fellow executives said was more than willing to "step on toes" to make changes, to get things moving. Even his greatest triumph, appearing regularly as Georgie Girl's sidekick in the pages of the *Insider's Report*, has not met unanimous enthusiasm. After Nichol bought Canadian rights to the idea from "Trader Joe" Coulombe, a California food and liquor retailer in 1983, he came in for his share of criticism for using Loblaws to satisfy his own craving for celebrity. In those days, "Trader Dave's" person could be seen not only in the *Insider's Report* but also in Loblaws' television commercials and in-store posters. He soon became known as "Mr. Ego" in the grocery business.

In 1985, when Nichol was unceremoniously dropped from his job as president of Loblaws Ontario Ltd. and put in charge of the newly created Loblaw International Merchants, it looked to many outsiders as if he had fallen from grace, as if Galen Weston's college room-mate was being expelled from the inner circle. In fact, Nichol's move wasn't a fall so much as a repositioning. Nichol was never an administrator or a numbers man like Currie, and it was clear that running Loblaws Ontario Ltd. after 1985 was going to be a job for someone immersed in controls and administration. It simply made more sense to use Nichol where his strong marketing talents were most appropriate, picking sexy goodies that would attract customers and then exploiting his strong personal appeal to close the sale.

Analyst Don Tigert of Toronto investment dealer Burns Fry Ltd. tells about a chance meeting with Nichol in the Loblaws' store at Lakeshore Boulevard and Leslie Street in Toronto. "I noticed he was in the pet food aisle," he recalls. "I asked him what he was doing there and he said that he was going to spend the day trying to figure out how to increase the gross margin on pet foods until it was 4% of sales. I asked him how he was going to do it. He said, 'Well, you've got national brands and private brands and a number of facings of each product. You can vary the shelves that you put them on. If you put something on the lowest shelf instead of the one nearest eye level the rate of sales can be four times different, even though the price remains the same.' Using point of sale scanning equipment he could see how many cans of Alpo or whatever would go through the checkout counter for a couple of hours. Then he could put the cans on another shelf. He's really down to the nitty gritty of the business."

It goes without saying that he can do the same for olives.

CHAPTER 11

Waiting for Garry

"Where significant profit opportunities are identified in areas relevant to our management skills and objectives, we plan to utilize part of our cash resources. In the present climate of uncertainty over the outlook for currency values and interest rates, I believe there is no shortage of time to meet these objectives."

Garry H. Weston, from the chairman's
statement to the shareholders of
Associated British Foods
Group, 1983

While Garfield Weston was, pound for pound, the most acquisitive and relentless deal maker in the history of Canadian business, his second son has enormous trouble when it comes to spending a buck. While the father once managed to gobble up something like 60 companies in a ten-year buying binge, Garry Weston has managed in his 20-year stint as ABF chairman to avoid making a single significant acquisition. Instead his specialty is the well-timed sale, an instinctive feel for the moment when an asset's value has peaked and it should be passed along. In this way, Weston has managed in the past four years to hive off faltering pieces of the vast conglomerate he inherited from his father and, in so doing, generated a pile of cash that at last report totalled roughly $2.5 billion. Given the possibility of leveraging this amount with debt borrowings, he could buy a company or companies worth at least twice that much — if only he could make up his mind about what he wants to buy.

While the stockbrokers of the City of London and Britain's largest institutional investors wait with bated breath to see what Weston will do with his swelling pile of cash, he does nothing to ease their anticipation and their mounting frustration. He sends no signals beyond obvious generalities, courts no casual advisors and ignores the rumour mill. When he makes public statements about ABF's affairs, usually to report on interim and annual sales and earnings figures, it's in prose that can only be described as the linguistic equivalent of ABF's top-selling Sunblest white sandwich loaf. If Weston were doing the official narration for the end of the world, he would make it seem a tedious event. For good measure, Weston sees that ABF's annual reports have a degree of consistency that extends well beyond the income statement and balance sheet. Every year for the past five, the chairman's picture — a slightly open-mouthed portrait in which Weston appears to be gritting his teeth — has remained unchanged. So in large part has the tribute to employee loyalty that traditionally rounds out the chairman's statement.

This seemingly calculated blandness meshes perfectly with Garry Weston's personal image. "What is work?" Weston once tossed back at a curious journalist. "I don't know where it begins or ends. It's an expression of one's personality." Coming from most CEOs, such a comment would be no more than an evasive banality. From Weston though, it is an important clue to his character. Lacking anything more, camp followers of ABF have felt compelled to turn Weston into an eccentric by default, to celebrate his relentless ordinariness to such an extent that it becomes interesting. Garry shops in his own stores, reportedly likes to take advantage of bargains when he sees them and is said to return substandard merchandise; he rides the tube and takes his shoes off at the office. Even his purported ability to remain anonymous at public functions commands attention; Garry Weston is the Zelig of British industry.

Much the same notion prevails in North America, particularly when he's compared to his father, Garfield, or his younger brother, Galen. "His father was a fantastically charismatic and inspirational guy," says a Bay Street veteran who has known all three men. "When Garfield Weston toured his factories, people told stories about him for days afterwards. Galen is a lot like him; he's his father's proper heir. Garry is regarded as the sober one, the accountant-type mentality, where Galen is a marketing-driven person. Galen would say, let's drive the business through the front door and figure out how to control the costs once we've got it. Garry would say, let's keep the costs low."

Given the growth with glitz that has characterized Galen's 14-year tenure in the chairmanship of Toronto's George Weston Ltd., and the more measured and quiet approach Garry Weston has taken at ABF, it's tempting to take this assessment at face value. Yet this would also denigrate Garry Weston's very real accomplishments for, while he most assuredly lacks glamour, he is just as legitimate a corporate heir as his brother. The classic pattern of a business' development is that its initial growth is driven and inspired by an entrepreneur, a visionary risk-taker who has the courage to take the chances that will produce results. But in the second, more mature phase of such a business, entrepreneurs often give way to professional managers. The emphasis now is not so much on breakneck growth as it is on the skilful rationalization and consolidation of the assets that have already been piled up. Expenditures are made to expand and improve production or distribution facilities. Cash flow from your established business and, if necessary, outside borrowings in the form of additional equity or debt are used to finance growth from within. The Weston empire conforms to this pattern, and Garry's role is not only logical, but desirable.

Garfield Weston parlayed a comparatively small investment made in 1934 in an Aberdeen bread and biscuit maker, Mitchell &

Muil, Ltd., into ABF, which, by the time Garry took the helm in early 1968, was a baking, milling and food retailing empire stretching over three continents and generating annual revenues of slightly more than $1 billion and profits of $44 million. Eighteen years later, in fiscal 1986, the company's sales were six times higher, at $6.4 billion, while profits were more than eight times greater, at a little more than $335 million. Weston did it by systematically investing in and developing the core baking and milling subsidiaries while selling major interests that were either about to go sour or were unlikely ever to experience strong revenue and profit growth rates. Or as analyst and current ABF booster David Lang of the London stockbroking firm Henderson Crossthwaite bluntly describes it: "He's put straight a lot of things his father screwed up." The irony, however, is that Garry's been so successful raising cash from well-timed disposals that he's been forced into what is for him the intensely uncomfortable role of a take-over artist.

Weston's first major disinvestment coup was the decision in the spring of 1983 to sell ABF's 52% controlling interest in the Premier Group Ltd. of South Africa for $710 million. After paying off debts totalling $325 million, the company had net cash proceeds of $385 million to invest in short-term securities. At first it looked like a huge mistake. ABF had had a significant stake in Premier Group since 1963 and Garfield Weston, as his infamous remarks in support of apartheid at the George Weston Ltd. 1964 annual meeting seemed to underline, certainly had a long-term commitment. Under Garry Weston's stewardship, this hardly diminished. If anything, it seemed to be increasing; between 1979 and 1983, Weston endorsed the local chairman, A.H. Bloom, in his plans to double annual capital spending to more than $600 million. This hardly seemed extravagant. Premier, with its diverse interests in baking, biscuits, milling, animal feeds, edible oils and pharmaceuticals, had increased profits more than 34% from 1980 to 1983 and had been a strong and steady contributor to ABF's bottom line. In 1983, roughly 17% or $45.5 million of ABF's $274 million in pretax profits came from South

Africa. The social fabric of the country was coming apart, but it was still in many ways a significant economic force, if only because it remained the world's largest gold producer. And for ABF and the host of other multinationals there, South Africa still provided attractive rates of return on investment.

Weston was only too well aware of the racial problem, and he publicly recognized the role companies like his would have to play in gradually leaning on the white government to change the system. As he put it, businesses would have to "take a lead in dismantling discrimination." He was also on the receiving end of periodic bids by South African business groups to buy back Premier in its entirety, but for a long time he was convinced that the group's profit record and growth potential would make it too rich for the locals' blood. But by March of 1983, with the ABF financial year drawing to a close, Weston had largely changed his mind on this score. The South African economy was becoming increasingly isolated and was now clearly in a severe recession. The rand, which had been worth roughly $1.50 in 1980, was now down to 90 cents and falling fast. Interest rates in the country were at historically high levels, and margins in Premier's key operating areas, notoriously thin at the best of times, were being pared to the bone. The proverbial final straw seemed to be news of a drought which reduced grain harvests and damaged operating returns in Premier's animal feed and milling subsidiaries. As Weston scanned the results coming in from Johannesburg, the bright spots were few and far between. One was the initial marketing success of a new range of dried pet food products; another was the healthy results of one of Premier's atypical offshoots, a music, publishing and home electrical distributor known as the Gallo Group.

By the time Weston was approached by a consortium headed by Johannesburg Consolidated Investment Co. and Liberty Life Association of Africa Ltd. early in 1983, hard-headed reality had set in. Suddenly he had a more profound understanding of the growing Afrikaner compulsion to repatriate assets. What's more, the consortium offered a price that, as he would later tell

ABF stockholders and creditors in a company circular, "reflects fully the value of the investment in Premier." And as he pointed out in the same circular, "given ABF's policy of retaining majority control in its overseas investments, the commitment of any further substantial additional funds in the form of both equity and loan capital would, in the view of your directors, have produced a disproportionate involvement in one economy relative to ABF's total spread of profit and assets." Undoubtedly, this ranks as a masterpiece of euphemistic corporate language, but perhaps Weston could be forgiven considering the other advantages that the deal had for ABF. One was that because of the way the sale was made, the proceeds wouldn't be subject to capital gains tax in either South Africa or Great Britain. And while the purchase price would be remitted over a six-month period, Weston could rest easy about any potential dilution in value that would come from a falling rand. Even though the South African Exchange Control Authorities had backed away from maintaining an official rate for the rand that February, the government was willing to hold to the old, stable rate for the purposes of this particular transaction.

In hindsight, the decision to sell Premier seems a brilliant one. The deterioration of the South African economy and currency has continued unabated, prompting more and more multinationals to get out and more and more countries to reduce or suspend trade. The country, now dominated by the cries of frustrated blacks and the paranoia of extremist whites, seems unable to solve its problems in any peaceable, orderly way. Any potential profits that ABF might have made by hanging on to Premier would have been more than compensated for by exchange problems and the exquisite discomfort that would befall a major international company that appeared to be supporting the world's number one pariah state.

There's scarcely been enough time to get the same perspective on Weston's second major addition to the coffers at ABF, the $1.4 billion sale in June, 1986, of the Fine Fare retail food chain to a slightly larger competitor, Dee Corp. Initially, his decision to sell was again surprising, given Fine Fare's history within the group and its profit contribution. ABF had built Fine Fare from scratch beginning in the early 1960s; it was to be the domestic base from which Garfield Weston would launch his Napoleonic retail sweep of the Continent. When it ran into problems caused by rapid expansion — lack of management skill, low turnover and ulti-mately losses on the bottom line — the elder Weston and his Canadian lieutenant, George Metcalf, mounted a major rescue effort, shifting ownership of the chain to George Weston Ltd. in order to infuse it with needed cash. The Canadian wing had even gone as far as infusing it with needed grocery retailing skills, shipping over groups of apprentice store managers.

In recent years, Fine Fare hadn't needed any help from the colonies. The chain had become the fastest-growing segment of ABF, achieving a 4.5% share of the U.K. grocery market. In fiscal 1986, despite the attendant costs of adding 13 new stores and closing down 32 older ones, the chain's profits had increased by almost 25%. It was overwhelmingly the largest contributor to ABF's U.K. retail operations in which revenues gained 45% and pretax profits rose 26% for the year. As late as the spring of 1986, Weston said he was forging ahead with plans to open 15 more stores as part of a program that "will ensure the highest capital spending in the history of the company."

By that time, however, Weston and his top managers must have recognized the potential folly of sticking to their ambitious plan. ABF certainly had the cash to build the chain, thanks to the sale of Premier Milling, but the real giants of British food retailing, J. Sainsbury and Tesco Ltd., had major expansion programs of their own. Given the already commanding lead they had in market share (Sainsburys had almost 12% of the market as of 1985 and Tesco was just slightly lower), it was unlikely ABF could ever spend enough to catch up. The other very real consideration was that Fine Fare's increasing success might be partially at the expense of ABF's baking and milling arms. The major chains were and are major customers of Allied Bakeries, for instance, and any move to build up Fine Fare might have induced these customer competitors to move to other suppliers such as Allied's archrival, Ranks Hovis McDougall.

These were the logical, market-based reasons for selling out, but many in the financial community believe there was another, more emotional and psychological basis for Weston's decision. "Garry Weston is essentially a production man rather than a marketing man," says analyst John Elston of City stockbroker James Capel. "You get the production right, the costs come down and you'll survive. So he invests in production facilities." It's one way of saying that Garry, like his grandfather George Weston, is more content with the idea of being an efficient baker and miller than a hustling retailer. Whatever his actual motivation, Weston and the sparse staff at ABF headquarters just off London's Hyde Park quietly negotiated with Dee, issuing the occasional denial that anything was happening and letting an active rumour mill churn ahead. The investment community started looking for a sale early in the year, particularly one that would transfer Fine Fare to the hands of James Gulliver, the brilliant Scots manager who had been rapidly promoted to the head of the chain by Garfield Weston in the mid-1960s.

Gulliver had left ABF in 1972, built up and then profitably sold a wholesale operation, Oriel Foods, and in 1979, had begun assembling a new food production and retailing conglomerate, Argyll Group. At one time, Gulliver had had an understanding with Garfield Weston that Fine Fare might be split off from ABF and that stock would be made available to senior executives. As Gulliver later commented, Garry Weston nixed that once he took over, simply because there was no compelling reason to let family control slip away. Now such a transfer of ownership would seem like destiny fulfilled. But it was not meant to be. In June, the pact with Dee was signed, giving ABF a mixture of cash and Dee shares. For good measure, Weston threw in another discount shopping chain, Shoppers Paradise, and a country club, the Bishop's Stortford Golf Club — a pleasant gesture from one whose main hobbies aside from work are said to be gardening and tennis.

There is such a thing as an embarrassment of riches and by late

1986, with its cash hoard running at about $1.8 billion, that's exactly what ABF faced. Under Britain's Income and Corporation Taxes Act, ABF was considered a "close company," in other words, a company in which more than 65% of the stock is controlled by five people or fewer or by five or fewer associated groups. In ABF's case, Wittington Investments Ltd., which Garry controls, held 71% of ABF's stock. The problem with this is that the Act requires that such companies distribute "unearned income" — interest and dividends — to shareholders. If the company doesn't, Inland Revenue will still go ahead and tax the shareholders as if it had been. In effect, ABF's shareholders, in particular Garry Weston and family, were about to be saddled with an enormous tax bill because of all the unearned income the cash pile was generating.

Once again there was much speculation in the City, this time that the family, through Wittington, might take the easy way out and sell just enough shares to get their holding down to 65%. But Weston thought otherwise. Simply reducing the family holding would have produced another nasty tax repercussion, this time in the form of a capital gains liability. What he did instead was arrange in early December to sell more than $300 million in new ABF shares. He invited investment dealers to make bids for a "bought deal" (they would buy the shares and take the risk of reselling them to institutions and retail buyers), eventually settling on a National Westminster Bank subsidiary, County Securities. The sale was enough to reduce the controlling stake to roughly 62%, avoid tax problems and, naturally, add to the war chest. The only problem that remained now was the seemingly insoluble one — what was he going to do with the cash?

Garry Weston has always had a keen appreciation of his own strengths and weaknesses. He's long been aware that he is not like his father. As he told *Business Week* more than a decade ago, "I don't have his flair. I'm not the leader he was. I need more of a structure to operate with. I've got to work through people." Certainly he has never been a publicity seeker. Whatever flair he indeed has, it is reserved for family and close associates.

Garry was born on April 28, 1927, in Toronto, Garfield and Reta Weston's fourth child in almost as many years, and the second son. His early life was one of abrupt changes, acted out first in Toronto, then at his father's rambling stone estate in Woodbridge, The Four Winds, and then on to Britain and the vast house at Marlow-on-Thames. Garry Weston's boyhood coincided with his father's peaking as an entrepreneur and it's easy to imagine that each passing month brought excitement, tension (especially in the late 1920s, when his father courted failure in his initial U.S. expansion) and a burgeoning sense of grandeur. Garry was a chunky youth, blue-eyed and with a great sweep of blond hair that was constantly in danger of falling over his face. He was given to wearing knee socks and sensible Oxfords, appropriate garb for a day boy at the Sir William Borlase School in nearby Marlow. He was strong academically and in fact is the only Weston male to approach being a scholar. By the time he'd grown into a tall, lean young man, he'd qualified for New College, Oxford, where he read economics. After that, he took an advanced economics degree at Harvard.

In 1947, fresh from Boston, he was inducted into the family business as a high-level management trainee. This didn't mean a plush office — he recalled that his first task was to help assemble a baking oven — but he moved from one subsidiary to another, learning the ropes. This lasted four years, a period that, looking back, he considered a "waste of time," because he hadn't really had any responsibility. This came in 1951 when his father made him chairman of ABF's Ryvita Co. subsidiary. Three years later, Garfield Weston sent him to Australia to start manufacturing crispbreads. While he was there, his father added, he might also see what he could do to reorganize and expand biscuit production that was already run by George Weston Foods. What initially looked like a few years in the outback became a 14-year career. In consultation with his father, Garry Weston broadened Australian interests not only in the traditional areas of baking, biscuit making and milling, but he also bought interests in businesses as diverse as furniture and bedding and wholesale meat and slaughter houses.

He also managed to find time for a personal life. In 1959, at the age of 32, he married 24-year-old Mary Ruth Kippenberger, daughter of the late Major-General Sir Howard Kippenberger, best known as the editor of New Zealand's official war histories. (Typically, Garfield Weston tried to interpret the marriage as a broad statement of family patriotism, noting that "we're doing everything possible to bring the Commonwealth together.") Garry, who soon after his wedding was appointed vice-chairman of ABF as well as holding on to his duties in Australia, did emulate his father in one respect: he settled down to produce a large family and fathered six children.

Eventually he was given the nod to take an active role in guiding the affairs of ABF. In early 1968, just before his second son's fortieth birthday, Garfield Weston announced that he was appointing Garry as the group's chairman. Henceforth Garry would be responsible for day-to-day operations while Garfield would retain the title of president and concentrate on long-range planning and policy-making. The son may have been overshadowed, but he wasn't overawed. He systematically began to get ABF back to basics and a well-thought-out program of internally generated expansion. Fine Fare, under Gulliver's direction, was coming out of the red, leaving Weston free to pull ABF out of some less fortunate diversification schemes. Among the sell-offs in his first several years at the helm were companies involved in making soft drinks, pet foods and plastics as well as an engineering services firm. The cash he received along with retained earnings he invested in long-time staples: baking, biscuits and milling. Between 1970 and 1975, for instance, he spent roughly $508 million to upgrade plant and equipment in ABF's primary businesses.

Along the way he developed a profound appreciation for the delicate politics and hazardous economics of bread making. Bread consumption went into decline after the Second World War — like potatoes by the Irish, bread has been viewed by the

British as a somewhat inferior food, to be avoided in a period of growing affluence — and has never really recovered. By 1970, British production was essentially confined to five major concerns, all of them intensely competitive. To complicate the picture, bread prices had been a traditional political football; periodically there were government controls and companies had to justify increases. One of the ways they did this was to point to the perennial woes caused by labour unions. When workers weren't moving on, giving their companies annual staff turnover rates of roughly 80%, they were pushing for better conditions and, in particular, fewer night shifts. George Weston himself would have appreciated the need for a baker to be a sharp operator under these circumstances, and certainly his grandson Garry did too. Weston's greatest coups seemed to be the ability to build better plants, put up more efficient flour mills — that could, for example, produce acceptable flours from British grains that weren't up to the quality of imported strains — and to invest in facilities that would make unexciting but useful related products such as starch and gluten, a plant protein mixture that can be substituted for flour.

Weston also made his influence felt on ABF's organization and operating style. While he kept the lean head office staff structure originated by his father, he became a much more hands-on manager. When he arrived at ABF headquarters on Barclay Square in the late sixties, the company network was a sprawling one. Management in most of the subsidiary operations largely went its own way, particularly if they were profitable. It was an Old Country parallel to the decentralized free-for-all that characterized George Metcalf's era at George Weston Ltd. and Loblaw Companies in Canada. As Garry commented a few years into his stewardship: "My father's business had no structure. There were at least a hundred people at ABF who thought they reported directly to Garfield Weston." For several years, Garry Weston redressed the balance by taking what many considered was too involved a role, making personal decisions on investments as small as $50,000 or $60,000.

Along the way, Weston earned a reputation as a thorough, tough-minded executive who was deliberative rather than impulsive, the very antithesis of his father. He also took on more depth for the outsiders from the City who dealt with him regularly. According to Henderson Crossthwaite's David Lang, who has known him for 15 years, Weston's image as a quirky eccentric is nothing more than a concoction of imaginative journalists. "They make him out as some sort of freak when he's anything but. He's such a normal individual," he says. "He's quite a private person, but he has a good sense of humour. He's not pompous; he'll share a joke with you. But he is a tremendous businessman. Just look at his profit record."

In fact, ABF has been a steady, but sometimes far from spectacular profit performer. For example, in 1984 pretax profits dipped sharply to $220 million from $275 million the year before. Arguably, results at times might have looked better were it not for the fact that ABF, at Weston's request, follows ultra-conservative accounting policies. Unlike other large firms with retail subsidiaries, for instance, ABF doesn't include profits from real estate dealings before it determines pretax earnings. Generally though, Garry's era at ABF has been one of rising fortunes, a fact reflected in the respect, if not always admiration and excitement, with which British investors view ABF's shares.

Naturally they'd view the shares with considerably more excitement if Weston would get on with the task of spending his money. And to his credit, he's been trying hard. Since mid-1985 he's looked at several options and has admitted making two offers, one for a U.K. business, the other for a U.S. operation. Neither came to fruition, but there has been no shortage of guesswork going on. One rumour has been that he would like to take over United Biscuits, the nation's largest producer with a 40% market share. Mainly through its subsidiary, Burton's Gold Medal Biscuits Ltd. of Blackpool, ABF already has about a 5% share of the U.K. biscuit market. The addition of United, the U.K.'s sixty-first largest company (interestingly enough, just after Jim Gulliver's Argyll Group) with annual sales of more than

$3.6 billion and pretax profits of more than $200 million, would give it a commanding position and the close attention of the Office of Fair Trading, the U.K. equivalent of Canada's Competition Tribunal. Yet, according to a profile of Garry Weston published last year by *Business Magazine* in the United Kingdom, he'd be rather unlikely to get along with United's chairman, Sir Hector Laing.

There have been other possibilities. ABF was rumoured as a suitor for the large brewing concern, Courage, one of the segments of Imperial Group, a food, drink, tobacco, hotel and catering conglomerate that's gradually been dismantled. Another story had Weston playing the role of white knight in a bidding war with Ranks Hovis McDougall (RHM) for another diversified food producer, Avana Group of Cardiff. In purely comestible terms, it would have amounted to a battle between Sunblest bread (ABF) and Bisto gravy mix (RHM) for control of Robertson's jam. So far though, Weston hasn't been enticed by such sweet prospects. He is, however, known to favour businesses he's already familiar with, and he has looked longingly at the United States, where ABF's interests to date are limited to a subsidiary that makes adhesives and a North Carolina tea plant run by R. Twining & Co. Ltd.

Which raises an interesting question. While Garfield Weston roamed the world at will, his corporate heirs seem to have divided things in two, both operationally and in terms of actual shareholding control. With a few minor exceptions (Galen Weston owns a Dublin department store, for example), North America is George Weston Ltd.'s turf, while Europe and Australia belong to ABF. Likewise, even though the brothers sit on each other's boards, Garry has ultimate personal control of ABF while Galen holds sway at George Weston Ltd. Under these circumstances then, would they act together on a major new thrust? According to one informed observer, that's fairly unlikely. "I don't see them getting into bed with each other," he says. "I get the impression they're doing their own things and that they wish to do so."

Garfield Weston once said that "the best thing that ever happened is that Galen is on one side of the ocean and Garry on the other." He simply meant that fate had been kind enough to grant him two capable sons who could manage his vast inheritance. He certainly wasn't, like some in the City, suggesting that the two boys would like an ocean's-width relationship for other reasons. Now, as ABF's cash pile swells to an even greater magnitude, it may be that Garry Weston has plans to change the territorial boundaries. And if he has, as usual he's keeping them to himself.

CHAPTER 12

Plus Ça Change

*"With God's help and guidance
'Tis not the gales, but the set of the sails
that determines the way you go.' "*

Inscription on Garfield Weston's memorial,
Mount Pleasant Cemetery, Toronto

To get to Constitution Hall in the basement of the Metro Toronto Convention Centre, you descend on a long escalator past a wall of mirrors that gives you more than enough time to make sure your tie is straight and your hair is combed. Yet on this particular day, a sunny Thursday in early May, the escalator is packed with richly tailored, impeccably coiffed analysts, institutional investors, bankers and stockbrokers, none of whom seem particularly interested in self-inspection. Like seagulls at a picnic ground, they project a kind of purposeful anticipation. They are here to attend one of the traditional highlights of the spring annual meeting circuit, the

George Weston Ltd. stockholders' gathering. At the bottom, in the long corridor outside the hall, Weston executives and directors mingle and chat with their public. People who are normally too busy to give you the time of day are there, relaxed and approachable, their working lives in limbo for this brief ritual pause. Only one of them, Wittington Investments Ltd. executive vice-president Roger Lindsay, seems the slightest bit apprehensive as he dispenses Weston lapel pins from a briefcase. Hilary Weston, looking ebullient in a peach-toned outfit, breaks through the crowd to laughingly demand her pin, and Lindsay obliges with a smile. Hilary's mood is that of the crowd. Within 30 seconds you can tell the company has had a good year simply by the tone of the jumbled conversational flow: the voices of the corporate officers are tinged with self-congratulation and pleasurable ease.

The talk becomes muted as people begin to drift into the dark and cavernous hall. No one has given a signal. People have simply looked at their Rolexes and Cartiers, noted that 11 A.M., the appointed hour, has arrived. The hall itself, normally a characterless concrete and steel bunker, has taken on such personality as the company and the convention centre's staff have deigned to give it. Red drapes have been hung on frames moved into place behind a long, raised head table with a podium that sits at the front of the hall. Behind and above the podium the Weston name is spelled out in large silver letters on the drapes: this typographical vestige of corporate culture is clean and modern, just like the smooth and efficient company it stands for. George Weston Ltd. knows how to project the image of a hard-driving corporation, just as it knows how to convey the rich tradition of a 105-year-old family-controlled company with folksy bread packaging.

Still, the visual minimalism of the annual meeting is a major break with tradition. Unlike George Weston Ltd. and Loblaw meetings in the 1960s, there are no Metcalfian blow-ups of prime rib roasts or steaks suspended from the ceiling. Nor are there the vast displays of Weston food products, as there were in the 1970s, waiting temptingly to be pillaged by legions of small shareholders at the adjournment of the meeting. In 1987, everything is under control; the goodies are in the 1986 annual reports and in the unexpectedly buoyant first quarter reports for the current year that the shareholders cling to their bosoms.

The directors sit along the head table in the soft warmth of overhead lights. Sitting on the far left, Dave Nichol majestically sweeps the crowd with his gaze and projects a Cheshire cat's self-confidence and serenity. Next to him Pauline McGibbon, retired Lieutenant-Governor of Ontario now turned corporate director, appears rigid and uncomfortable. Closer still to the podium Richard Currie sits motionless, his eyes focussed on some invisible spot over the heads of the audience. To the right of the podium sit less recognizable directors, including Hugo Mann, the managing director of Deutscher Supermarkt, the West German chain in which George Weston Ltd. has an interest, and Dr. Robert Mitchell, a surgeon who is an associate professor of medicine at the University of Toronto, a director of the Eye Research Institute and husband of Galen Weston's sister Barbara. The one notable no-show is Garry Weston, who heads the European and Australian wings of the family empire, Associated British Foods. Across a roughly 20-foot gulf the audience isn't quite so thoughtfully arranged, although there is an element of organization. In the second row of the centre section — by unspoken agreement it seems, nobody sits in the front row — Hilary Weston and an assortment of Weston aunts, uncles and cousins await the chairman's pleasure. Behind them, in no particular order, are the moneymen, the large investors and the usual healthy sprinkling of seniors who have held George Weston Ltd. stock for decades.

They used to come to see Garfield Weston perform his yearly bread and dreams number, that artful mixture of Babbittry and sociopolitical musings that could shock and amaze, but most of all convinced them that all was right with the world and their common shares. Now they come to see his son Galen provide the same reassurance and he doesn't disappoint. Without any ado, Weston takes to the podium and calls the meeting to order. He moves briskly through the time-honoured rituals of such occasions, receiving the financial statements for the previous year, electing directors and appointing auditors, all done with pre-arranged seconders and a total absence of criticism or fuss. These days George Weston Ltd. keeps no big secrets from its shareholders. It is a disclosure-minded company that often wins praise for the frankness of its annual reports.

The housekeeping done, Weston moves smoothly into his chairman's statement, the Bay Street equivalent of a sermon. One by one, he itemizes George Weston Ltd.'s accomplishments in its fifty-ninth year as a public company, its $10 billion sales in 1986, its return on investment and, above all, its increased dividend flow. This will not dry up because the company is planning and investing for the future by building new and bigger stores and adding to and rationalizing its food processing activities. And the company will remain profitable until these new operations mature because it has balanced strengths, such as resource earnings from paper and fisheries that will counteract any decline in food retailing activities. There's even a bit of carefully injected levity when Weston comments on the potential combined strength of the company's major candy producer, William Neilson Ltd., and the recently acquired Cadbury Schweppes Canada Inc. "We can do great things for both the Neilson and Cadbury product lines by putting the Crispy Crunch, Sweet Marie and your other favourites together with the Caramilk and the Crunchy," he exhorts. "We are now capable and determined to be not only the best but the biggest in this field — Wonderbar and Mars be warned."

As he delivers the statement, sometimes drawing out the ends of words with a slight British cadence, you become aware that the lighting in the hall has somehow managed to deepen the lines of his face, to highlight his cheekbones and the bridge of his nose. This, along with his increasingly grey hair, makes him look more like his father by the minute. And when he launches into the meat of his remarks, the impression becomes complete. Weston tells his shareholders that last year, at the convocation exercises at his old school, the University of Western Ontario, he spoke on the topic of free trade with the United States. He believes a free-trade agreement, now being negotiated on Canada's behalf by former George Weston Ltd. director Simon Reisman, is in the country's best interests. There will be dislocations and people and industries that need protection, he admits, but Canada needs such an agreement in order to have access to markets and to remain competitive. The alternative is increasing insularity and a diminished living standard.

On one level, Weston seems to be juggling with old family sentiments. He argues that Canadian sovereignty under a free trade pact need be no more jeopardized than that of the members of the European Economic Community. As he puts it, "Are the British less British" for having joined the EEC? Once upon a time, his father certainly would have answered yes and then he would have administered a tongue-lashing to the person impertinent enough to ask the question in the first place. Conventional wisdom changes, however, and so do notions of patriotism. The British Empire is dead, except on "Masterpiece Theatre"; the Commonwealth is a shell that serves mostly to embarrass its adherents with the gross discrepancies between its rich and poor members; and no one lately has suggested that able-bodied young men from the colonies ought to go and do their bit for Thatcher's Britain. Galen Weston may sound as if he's contradicting something that Garfield Weston held dear, but what he's really doing is confirming the more important lesson he learned at his father's knee, namely that true internationalism consists of bold and skilful entrepreneurship more than it does of antique notions of sovereignty and nationalism.

The other point of comparison is that Galen Weston, like his father, has been serving notice that he would like to be thought of as something more than a businessman, albeit a supremely successful one who happens to own castles in several countries. As was true of his father, there's a palpable yearning to take a stand on the major issues of our time and perhaps make a difference in the way people perceive them. There also seems to be a yearning for the grand gesture, the big project that can transcend the ordinary. Garfield Weston built Frenchman's Cove in Jamaica: now his son is thinking of sponsoring a $750 million commercial and residential real estate development in a northern suburb of Toronto that would feature a 100-storey building. The site, now occupied by a printing plant owned by media conglomerate Maclean Hunter Ltd., could become a lasting monument.

There isn't any reason why Galen Weston shouldn't be able to do all this and much more. Like his father he believes that if you have faith, resources, and most importantly, the will, you can do just about anything, an attitude nicely summed up by the message carved in the stone of the family's other monument, the one over Garfield Weston's grave. The line " 'Tis not the gales, but the set of your sails that determines the way you go," was adapted from the inscription on a painting of a storm-tossed ship that Garfield Weston owned most of his adult life and was a focal point of his many homes. The actual author of the line that became, in effect, Garfield Weston's "Rosebud" was a late nineteenth-century American poet, Ella Wheeler Wilcox. She was a prolific writer best known for her romantic and mildly erotic passages, and she made her point about sail-setting in an uplifting poem called "Winds of Fate." As Galen Weston increasingly follows the course his father set, the poem's message of self-determination takes on a renewed significance. The message may be subtler in the third generation of the family business, but it is still there. Underneath the modern, efficient and ruthlessly stylish shell is a soft centre of middle-class sentimentality.

This middle-class ethos is something that stockholders understand about the company and the family that runs it. In the end, the cool formality with which Galen Weston conducts a meeting is about as thin as the chocolate coatings on his father's cookies. Weston ends his thoughtful argument on the need for free trade, abruptly turning to a recap of the company's surprisingly buoyant first-quarter results. Then he throws the floor open for questions. Will the small shareholders want to know his views on the extent of industrial dislocation that could come under free trade? Will they bombard him with 1970s style economic nationalism and criticize him as a sell-out? Will they want to know if he has had any special insights from his friend, free trade negotiator Simon Reisman? Not at all. One man wants to talk about the method of dividend payment while an elderly woman asks what the company's plans are for an abandoned Loblaws' store on Pacific Avenue in Toronto's west end. The site is served by not one but three bus lines, and she thinks it would make a good place to build some needed senior citizens' housing. This same lady thinks George Weston Ltd. ought to be doing more to encourage consumers not to eat junk food and that the annual meeting should be moved back to its traditional venue, the Royal York Hotel's Canadian Room, so that people like her will never have to face inclement weather to get there. For good measure, she also wants to know if Loblaws will have a snack bar at the Canadian National Exhibition this year. There wasn't one last year, and she misses it.

Weston listens carefully and takes pains to deal with each question with courtesy and tact. Then, unwaveringly, he brings the meeting to a close, playing out a script that has worked for almost six decades. The only real change these days is the pace. Under his grandfather's and father's reigns, George Weston Ltd. meetings could drag out for more than an hour. This one is adjourned at 30 minutes, exactly.

Chronology

1865 - George Weston born in Oswego, New York.

1869 - Weston's family moves to Toronto.

1882 - George Weston goes into business on his own after buying two bread routes from G.H. Bowen.

1897 - The Model Bakery opens.

1898 - Garfield Weston born.

1900 - George Weston enters Model Bakery partnership with miller Lawrence Spink.

1905 - Model Bakery partnership dissolved. Company is wound up two years later.

1911 - George Weston merges his bakery interests into the newly formed Canada Bread Co. His biscuit factory is held separately.

1917 - Garfield Weston leaves high school and enlists in the Canadian Army Engineers and goes overseas.

1919 - Garfield Weston returns from France and begins work in his father's biscuit plant.

1920 - George Weston severs his connection with Canada Bread Co.

1922 - Garfield Weston introduces "English Style" biscuits to the Canadian market.

1924 - George Weston dies.

1927 - Garry Weston born.

1928 - George Weston Ltd. incorporated as a federal, public company. The company's profits in its first year are $168,000. Garfield Weston begins acquiring biscuit and confectionery companies in Canada as well as making his first investment in U.S. biscuit production.

1931 - Garfield Weston sells the old family baking business to the public company he controls.

1933 - Garfield Weston makes his first U.K. investment, buying biscuit maker Mitchell & Muil Ltd. of Aberdeen.

1935 - Garfield Weston takes up residence in the U.K.

1937 - George Weston Ltd. buys control of biscuit maker McCormick's Ltd. of London, Ontario.

1939 - Garfield Weston elected to the British Parliament after running unopposed in the Midlands riding of Macclesfield.

1940 - Galen Weston born.

1942 - Garfield Weston's one and only speech in the House of Commons.

1943 - Weston buys controlling interest in E.B. Eddy Co. Ltd. from Viscount Bennett.

1944 - George Weston Ltd. buys control of Western Grocers Ltd., a Winnipeg food wholesaler that is the precursor of Westfair Foods Ltd.

1947 - Garfield Weston acquires all of candy-maker William Neilson Ltd. of Toronto. That same year, through George Weston Ltd., he begins acquiring stock in Loblaw Groceterias. George Metcalf is hired away from Neilson by Loblaws to be a vice-president.

1951 - Garfield Weston buys control of Fortnum & Mason Ltd.

1952 - Wittington Investments Ltd. is incorporated as a private investment company by Garfield Weston. Shortly after, he transfers his controlling interest in George Weston Ltd. to this company. Subsequently, control of Wittington will pass to the W. Garfield Weston Charitable Foundation, a situation that will persist almost until the mid-1980s, when Galen Weston takes control of Wittington.

1954 - George Metcalf becomes president and managing director of George Weston Ltd. and embarks on a major acquisition campaign that will run until 1967. Garry Weston goes to Australia as managing director of Weston Biscuit Co.

1955 - Loblaw Groceterias gains 100% ownership of The O.K. Economy Stores Ltd. of Saskatoon and National Grocers Co. Ltd.

1956 - George Weston wins control of Loblaw Groceterias. Loblaw Companies Ltd. incorporated to hold this and other interests.

1959 - George Weston Ltd. wins voting control of Kelly Douglas & Co. of Vancouver. This same year, Loblaw Groceterias gets control of Atlantic Wholesalers of Sackville, New Brunswick, and Dionne Ltée. of Montreal.

1960 - Allied Bakeries Ltd. is renamed Associated British Foods and Garry Weston is appointed vice chairman.

1961 - Associated British Foods begins developing a new U.K. supermarket chain, Fine Fare.

1962 - Associated British Foods buys a 45% stake in the West German supermarket chain, Deutscher Supermarkt Handels-GmbH.

1963 - George Weston Ltd. gains control of National Tea. Associated British Foods buys a 51% stake in Premier Milling Co. of South Africa as well as a 94% share of a small French supermarket chain, Entrepôts Dubuffet. In the United Kingdom ABF puts the brakes to Fine Fare's expansion. In Australia, Garfield Weston buys a major baking and milling firm, W. Thomas Proprietary Ltd.

1966 - Under questioning from a Senate/Commons committee investigating food prices, Loblaw Companies officials agree to provide information concerning the company's various corporate connections.

1967 - Garry Weston becomes chairman of Associated British Foods; Garfield Weston retains the presidency. In Canada, Keith Dalglish is appointed vice-president and managing director of George Weston Ltd.

1969 - Keith Dalglish is replaced by George Creber as president of George Weston Ltd.

1972 - Galen Weston becomes chief executive officer of Loblaw Companies, replacing George Metcalf, who temporarily retains the chairmanship. Weston begins a radical consolidation and paring of company assets in order to improve sagging operating results.

1974 - Galen Weston becomes chairman and managing director of George Weston Ltd., replacing George Creber, who temporarily stays on as president.

1976 - George Weston Ltd., badly damaged by Loblaw Companies' efforts to turn around, posts its first ever loss, a shortfall of $15 million.

1978 - Garfield Weston, aged 80, dies in Toronto.

1983 - IRA kidnap attempt on Weston family in Ireland. Associated British Foods sells its now 52% holding in South Africa's Premier Group.

1985 - Loblaw Companies embarks on a four-year, $1.4-billion capital spending program that will gradually upgrade and expand its retail space.

1986 - Associated British Foods sells its U.K. supermarket chain, Fine Fare, to Dee Corp. A new share issue reduces family control of ABF to 62% from 71%. Galen Weston buys high fashion retailer Holt Renfrew Ltd. George Weston Ltd.'s sales break the $10-billion mark while net profits hit $119 million.

APPENDIX A

The Weston Family Tree

William Weston (1820-Nov. 5, 1900)
m. Ann Weston (1825-June 11, 1895)

Seven children, including

George Weston (March 23, 1865-April 6, 1924)
m. Emma Maud Richards (June 30, 1870-May 1, 1941)

Four sons and two daughters, including

Willard Garfield Weston (Feb. 26, 1898-Oct. 22, 1978)
m.1 Reta Lila Howard (July 4, 1897-March 17, 1967)
m.2 Marguerite Martin de Montoya

Six daughters and three sons from the
first marriage, including

Garfield Howard (Garry) Weston
(April 28, 1927-)
m. Mary Ruth Kippenberger
Three sons, three daughters

Willard G. Galen Weston
(Oct. 29, 1940-)
m. Hilary Mary Frayne
One son, one daughter

APPENDIX B: THE WESTON FAMILY'S NORTH AMERICAN HOLDING

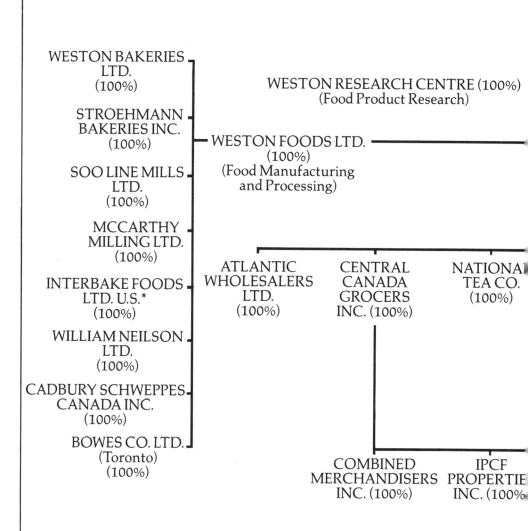

WESTON BAKERIES
LTD.
(100%)

STROEHMANN
BAKERIES INC.
(100%)

SOO LINE MILLS
LTD.
(100%)

MCCARTHY
MILLING LTD.
(100%)

INTERBAKE FOODS
LTD. U.S.*
(100%)

WILLIAM NEILSON
LTD.
(100%)

CADBURY SCHWEPPES
CANADA INC.
(100%)

BOWES CO. LTD.
(Toronto)
(100%)

WESTON RESEARCH CENTRE (100%)
(Food Product Research)

WESTON FOODS LTD.
(100%)
(Food Manufacturing
and Processing)

ATLANTIC
WHOLESALERS
LTD.
(100%)

CENTRAL
CANADA
GROCERS
INC. (100%)

NATIONAL
TEA CO.
(100%)

COMBINED
MERCHANDISERS
INC. (100%)

IPCF
PROPERTIE
INC. (100%

*INTERBAKE CANADA WAS SOLD THIS
SPRING TO NABISCO BRANDS LTD.

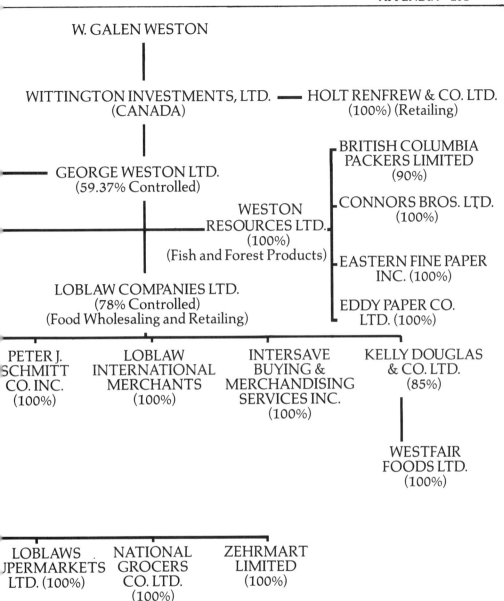

W. GALEN WESTON

WITTINGTON INVESTMENTS, LTD. — HOLT RENFREW & CO. LTD.
(CANADA) (100%) (Retailing)

GEORGE WESTON LTD.
(59.37% Controlled)

WESTON
RESOURCES LTD.
(100%)
(Fish and Forest Products)

BRITISH COLUMBIA
PACKERS LIMITED
(90%)

CONNORS BROS. LTD.
(100%)

EASTERN FINE PAPER
INC. (100%)

EDDY PAPER CO.
LTD. (100%)

LOBLAW COMPANIES LTD.
(78% Controlled)
(Food Wholesaling and Retailing)

PETER J.
SCHMITT
CO. INC.
(100%)

LOBLAW
INTERNATIONAL
MERCHANTS
(100%)

INTERSAVE
BUYING &
MERCHANDISING
SERVICES INC.
(100%)

KELLY DOUGLAS
& CO. LTD.
(85%)

WESTFAIR
FOODS LTD.
(100%)

LOBLAWS
SUPERMARKETS
LTD. (100%)

NATIONAL
GROCERS
CO. LTD.
(100%)

ZEHRMART
LIMITED
(100%)

APPENDIX C: THE WESTON FAMILY'S FOREIGN EMPIRE

EUROPE AND U.S.

TWINING CROSFIELD
GROUP (100%)
—9 Tea and Coffee
Factories

AUSTRALIA AND NEW ZEALAND

GEORGE WESTON
FOODS GROUP
(100%)
—22 Bakeries, 16 Mills,
5 Biscuit Factories as
Well as 18 Other
Companies

WHOLE OR PARTIAL OWNERSHIP OF 23 OTHER COMPANIES
INVOLVED IN FOOD PROCESSING, RETAILING, CONSTRUCTION,
OIL EXPLORATION, ADHESIVES AND RESEARCH.

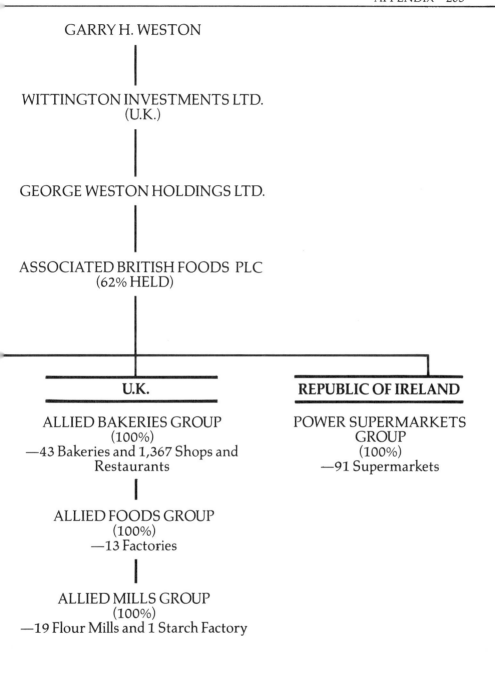

GARRY H. WESTON

WITTINGTON INVESTMENTS LTD.
(U.K.)

GEORGE WESTON HOLDINGS LTD.

ASSOCIATED BRITISH FOODS PLC
(62% HELD)

U.K.

ALLIED BAKERIES GROUP
(100%)
—43 Bakeries and 1,367 Shops and
Restaurants

ALLIED FOODS GROUP
(100%)
—13 Factories

ALLIED MILLS GROUP
(100%)
—19 Flour Mills and 1 Starch Factory

REPUBLIC OF IRELAND

POWER SUPERMARKETS
GROUP
(100%)
—91 Supermarkets

Index

A

A & P, 15, 156
A.B. Hemmings Ltd., 106
Advertising, 16, 74, 168
Aerated Bread Co. Ltd., 105
Aitken William Maxwell, 1st
   Baron Beaverbrook. *See*
   Beaverbrook, Lord
Allied Bakeries Ltd. *See*
   Associated British Foods
   Ltd.
Ashbourne, Mrs. Ernest. *See*
   Weston, Beatrice
Associated British Foods Ltd.
   (ABF), 71, 105-106, 112,
   118, 173, 176-181, 183
Atkins, Mabel. *See* Metcalf,
   Mrs. Charles
Atlantic Wholesalers, 5, 99

B

Bailey, Harold W., 12
Baker, Neil, 132
Bank of Nova Scotia, 59
Basford, Ron, 121
Bathurst Street Methodist
   Church, 48-50, 56

Battle of Britain, 81
B.C. Packers Ltd., 152
Beaverbrook, Lord, 64, 81-83
Bennett, R.B., 83
Berlin, Irving, 75
Bodley, Charles, 40
Bogue, Elizabeth, 60
Bowen, G.H., 21
Bread and baked goods
   industry
   in Britain, 53, 64, 69-71,
      75-76, 183-184
   in Canada, 20, 21, 39, 45,
      54, 62
   and technological
      revolution, 39-40, 44
Break, Pain and Wall Ltd., 154
Bredin, Mark, 43, 44-45, 48
Breadmen, 21-22
British Bakeries, 76
Brown, Thomas & Co. Ltd., 9

C

Canada Bread Co. Ltd., 43-46
Canada Food Board, 45
Carman United Church, 89
Chalmers, Floyd, 77

Chamberlain, Neville, 80
"Combination" stores, 170
Connell, Philip, 141
Connors Bros. Ltd., 137
Co-operative Retail Societies,
  76
Cooper and Co. Stores Ltd.,
  105
Co-operative Wholesale
  Society, 76
Cork, J. Milton, 91, 92-94, 96,
  97
Corporate Foods Ltd., 45
Creber, George Edgar (Ted),
  11, 141-147
Croll, David, 121
Crowther, W.H., 41
Cullen, Michael J., 95
Currie, Richard, 12, 154

D
Dalglish, Keith, 11, 137-141
*Dave Nichol's Insider's
  Report*, 14, 165, 166, 169
Davidge, Ernest, 56
Davidson, Brian, 13
Dee Corp., 180
de Montoya, Marguerite
  Martin. *See* Weston, Mrs. W.
  Garfield
Depression, 62-65, 94
Deutscher Supermarkt
  Handels-GmbH, 108
Dicoa Ltd., 112, 118
Dionne Ltée, 99
Dominion Stores Ltd., 15,
  148-149, 166
Dunne, Ben, 3

E
Eastern Fine Paper Inc., 152

E.B. Eddy Forest Products,
  16-17, 83
Entrepôts Dubuffet, 109
European Common Market,
  108, 109

F
Fine Fare (Holdings) Ltd.,
  106, 107, 111-114, 118,
  178-179
Food City, 149
Food prices, 120-121, 146,
  148-149, 156, 167
  1966 Senate/House
    Committee inquiry into,
    121-130, 133-134
Food retailing
  in Canada, 14, 15-16, 17-18,
    98-99, 120-121, 149,
    166-169
  in United Kingdom,
    106-107
  in United States, 94-95,
    106, 151, 156
Food Securities Ltd., 105
Food wholesalers, 98-99
Forest industry in Canada, 17
Fort Belvedere (Weston
  residence), 3
Fortnum & Mason Ltd.,
  66-67, 84, 102-104, 105
Frayne, Hilary. *See* Weston,
  Mrs. Willard Galen
Frenchman's Cove resort,
  115-116
Frogley, Charles J., 19

G
Garda, Irish anti-terrorist
  police, 3
George Weston Biscuit Co.,
  62

George Weston Bread &
  Cakes Ltd., 61, 63
George Weston Foods Ltd.,
  110
George Weston Holdings, 131
George Weston Ltd., 6, 10, 14,
  18, 62-65, 111, 113, 132,
  147. *See also individual
  subsidiaries*
  corporate culture, 123
  corporate disclosure, 133,
    139, 144, 146-147
  expansion under Galen
    Weston, 11-14, 15, 17, 157,
    186
  expansion under W.
    Garfield Weston, 58-59,
    61-62, 63-65, 67-72, 83,
    84, 104-111, 131, 136
  food distribution division,
    14, 15, 17, 151
  food processing division,
    10, 13, 17, 152
  resources division, 14,
    16-17, 152
  retail division, 152
Glenhuron Properties Ltd.,
  153
Gold, Abe, 140
Grain export, 75, 76
G. Tamblyn Ltd., 10, 152
Guards Polo Club, 3
Gulliver, James, 114, 180

H
Haynes, Ernest, 77
Holt Renfrew Ltd., 15
Horne & Pitfield Foods Ltd.,
  145
"House" brands, 16, 17, 169
Howard, Reta Lila. *See*

Weston, Mrs. W. Garfield
Howardsgate Holdings Ltd.,
  112
Hudson's Bay Co., 160-162
Hunter, Horace T., 77

I
Income and Corporation
  Taxes Act (British), 181
*Insider's Report. See Dave Nichol's
  Insider's Report*
Irish Republican Army (IRA)
  kidnap attempt, 1-4

J
Jamaica Queen (cruise ship), 116

K
Kane, William J., 156
Keedoozle Stores, 95
Kelly Douglas & Co., 5, 99,
  126-127
Keppenberger, Mary Ruth. *See*
  Weston, Mrs. Garry
King Kullen (store), 95
Krysiak, F. Bruce, 151,
  155-156

L
Lawlor's Bread, 63
Lindsay, Roger, 12
Loblaw, Theodore Pringle,
  92-94, 95-96, 123
Loblaw Companies Ltd., 5,
  10-13, 97, 132, 136, 147,
  157, 166
  1971 financial crisis,
    153-154
  1972-1975 reorganization,
    11-13, 154, 171
  1985 capital spending

program, 169-170
Loblaw Groceterias Co., 5, 10,
    11, 15, 17, 86, 91, 97, 131
    founding of, 92-94
    growth of, 94, 96, 98-99,
    137
    unionization of, 124
    decline of, 149
    reorganization of, 154-155
Loblaw Inc., 98, 137
Loblaw International
    Merchants Ltd., 5, 165
Loeb, Bertram, 145

M
Maple Leafs polo squad, 3-4
Marks & Spencer, 169
McNamara, Harley V., 150
Meech, Richard G., 121-130
Metcalf, Charles, 87-88
Metcalf, Mrs. Charles (née
    Mabel Atkins), 87
Metcalf, George, 10, 85
    appearance, 86, 88
    management style, 86, 87,
    99, 143
    education, 88
    first jobs, 88-90
    recreation, 88, 89
    Carman United Church, 89
    marriage to Victoria
    Waring, 89
    career at William Neilson
    Ltd., 90-91
    career at Loblaws, 91, 98,
    99-101, 141, 152
    career at George Weston
    Ltd., 86, 99, 133, 157
Metcalf, Mrs. George (née
    Victoria Waring), 89
Miracle Food Marts, 149

Mitchell & Muil Ltd., 70
M. Loeb Ltd., 144-145
Model Bakery, 40-41, 42, 43,
    46
Morden, C.R., 41-42
Mr. Grocer, 15
Mulock, Cawthra, 42-44

N
National brands, 168
National Grocers Co. Ltd., 99
National Tea Co., 10, 12, 98,
    106, 137, 150-151, 155, 157
N.B. Love Industries Ltd., 110
"Neilson Hour," 90
Neilson, Morden, 91
Nichol, David, 9, 12-13, 154,
    164-166, 170, 171-172
Nuffield, Lord, 68

O
Ontario Bakeries Ltd., 63-64

P
Penney's (department store),
    9
Pentland, Bill, 55-56
Pezim, Murray, 142-143
Piggly Wiggly Store, 95
Power Supermarket
    (Canada), 140
Power Supermarket (Ireland),
    9
Premier Group Ltd., 176-177
Premier Milling Co. Ltd.,
    110-111. *See also*
    Premier Group Ltd.
President's Choice private
    label, 14, 166, 169
Price wars, 148-149, 156, 157,
    167

R
Rank, Joseph, 73
Rank and Spillers, 75-76
Regal Bakeries, 63
Reisman, Simon, 12
Richards, Emma Maud. *See*
 Weston, Mrs. George
Robertson, Mrs. Stanley. *See*
 Weston, Pearl
Rothermere, Lord, 64
Roundwood Park (Weston
 residence), 3, 4
Royal Commission on
 Corporate Concentration,
 98, 100
Royal Commission on Price
 Spreads of Food Products,
 120

S
Sainsbury, J., 179
Saltsman, Max, 121
Saunders, Clarence, 95
Sayvette Ltd., 10, 140-141,
 152
Shelley, Ben, 113
Smith, Bernard E., 65, 77
Spink, Lawrence, 40, 41
Stepelton, Norman A., 150,
 151
Stewart, David, 17
Steinberg's Miracle Food
 Marts, 149
Sullivan, Joe, 3
Super Carnaval, 16
Supermarkets, 95, 106-107,
 167
Superstores, 15, 17, 18, 167

T
Teddy's Choice private label,
 169

Terrorism and business
 people, 4
Thomson, Kenneth, 161-162
Thornton-Smith, Ernest, 84
Tigert, Donald, 98, 100, 171
Toronto, 22, 42, 48, 50
Trading stamps, 113, 120

U
United Bakeries, 76
United Biscuits, 185
Urie, John J., 126-130

V
Vickers & Benson, 154
Vitbe Flour Mills, 106

W
Warehouse club stores, 16
Waring, Victoria. *See*
 Metcalf, Mrs. George
Watson, James A., 12, 157
Watt, Don, 11, 154
Weinstein, Leon, 140
"Wellness generation,"
 167-168
Western Grocers Ltd., 83
Westfair Foods, 5
Weston, Alfred J., 40, 121
Weston, Beatrice (Mrs. Ernest
 Ashbourne), 62
Weston Biscuit Co., 55
Weston Biscuit Co.
 (Australia), 110
Weston, Garry, 5, 8, 84, 110,
 159
 CEO of ABF, 173-174,
  183-187
 public image, 174-175, 185
 management style, 175,
  181, 184

Premier Group Ltd. sale,
  176-178
Fine Fare sale, 178-179
recreation, 180
education, 182
first jobs, 182
marriage to Mary Ruth
  Kippenberger, 183
Weston, Mrs. Garry (née
  Mary Ruth Kippenberger),
  183
Weston, George, 4, 19, 54
  education, 20
  apprenticeship, 20-21
  purchase of bread routes,
    22
  appearance, 22
  Model Bakery, 40-41, 42, 43
  management style, 39
  Canada Bread, 43
  marriage to Emma Maud
    Richards, 47
  residences, 47
  election as Ward Four
    alderman, 48
  Bathurst Street Methodist
    Church, 48-50
  death, 51
Weston, Mrs. George (née
  Emma Maud Richards), 47
Weston, Gordon, 50, 61
Weston, Grainger, 8, 115, 116
Weston, Pearl (Mrs. Stanley
  Robertson), 59, 62
Weston, Willard Galen
  IRA kidnapping attempt,
    1-3, 4
  residences, 3, 4
  recreation, 3-4, 10
  personal wealth, 6
  management style, 6, 11-
    12, 14, 18, 175
  charities, 7
  appearance, 7
  education, 8, 9
  first jobs, 8
  Power Supermarket
    (Ireland), 9
  marriage to Hilary Frayne,
    9-10
  CEO of Loblaw Companies,
    153
  Loblaw Companies
    reorganization, 11-14, 154
  Holt Renfrew purchase, 15
  Loblaws expansion, 15, 17
  National Tea
    reorganization, 157
  CEO of George Weston
    Ltd., 157, 186
  Hudson's Bay Co. takeover
    attempt, 160-163
Weston, Mrs. Willard Galen
  (née Hilary Frayne), 9-10,
  15
Weston, Willard Garfield, 4, 5,
  50
  management style, 8, 61,
    68, 69, 72, 104-105
  relationship with children,
    8, 79
  appearance, 52, 61, 73-74
  First World War
    experiences, 52-53, 58
  apprenticeship, 54, 58
  birth, 55
  youth, 56
  education, 57
  George Weston Ltd.
    expansion, 58-59, 61-62,
      63-65, 66-72, 83, 84, 91,
      104-106, 108-111

marriage to Reta Lila
  Howard, 59-60
recreation, 60, 117, 158
physical breakdown, 62
Fortnum & Mason Ltd.,
  66-67, 84, 102-104
life in Britain, 67, 69, 78
Allied Bakeries Ltd., 71, 105
public relations skills,
  68-69, 73, 74
management skills, 74-76
and organized labour, 76
residences, 78-79, 83,
  135-136, 182
as British member of
  Parliament, 79-80
Second World War
  experiences, 80-83
E.B. Eddy Company, 83
and George Metcalf, 86, 90,
  91, 97
Loblaw Companies Ltd., 97
Fine Fare (Holdings) Ltd.,
  106, 107, 111
Entrepôts Dubuffet, 109
Premier Milling Co. Ltd.,
  110-111
student exchange program,
  115
Frenchman's Cove resort,
  115-116
public image, 73, 114, 116,
  144, 159
views on apartheid,

116-117
charities, 117, 158-159
death, 158
Weston, Mrs. W. Garfield (née
  Reta Lila Howard) (first
  wife), 59-60, 78-79, 118
Weston, Mrs. W. Garfield (née
  Marguerite Martin de
  Montoya) (second wife),
  158
Weston, William, 20-21
W. Garfield Weston
  Charitable Foundation,
  7, 117
Whelan, Eugene, 146
White, Jim, 169
Whittington (Weston
  residence), 78-79
Wholesale & Multiple
  Federation of Master
  Bakers, 76
William Neilson Co., 84,
  88-91
William Paterson Ltd., 62
Wittington Investments Ltd.,
  131, 153, 160, 181
Wittington Realty &
  Construction Ltd., 154
W. Thomas Industries
  Proprietary Ltd., 110

Z
Zehrs, 5

Acknowledgements

While writing this book I was fortunate to meet many people associated with the Weston family and companies who generously shared their memories and observations of this truly extraordinary Canadian business dynasty. There were also many others who, while not directly connected to the story, offered assistance out of an enthusiasm to flesh out a pocket of business history before much of the detail slips away along with the original players. To all those who gave freely of their time and knowledge I am deeply grateful.

Finally, I want to express my gratitude to my wife and children. During the writing of this book they had to live with a man obsessed and be truly supportive and loving at the same time. I cannot thank them enough.

CMD
July, 1987